PASTA

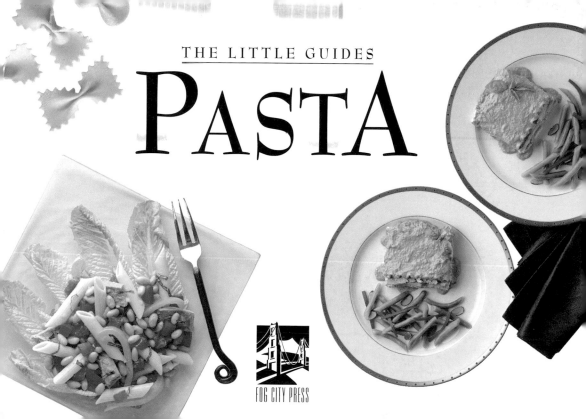

THE LITTLE GUIDES

PASTA

FOG CITY PRESS

Published by Fog City Press
814 Montgomery Street
San Francisco, CA 94133 USA
Reprinted in 2000 (twice), 2001

Chief Executive Officer: John Owen
President: Terry Newell
Publisher: Sheena Coupe
Associate Publisher: Lynn Humphries
Art Director: Sue Burk
Managing Editor: Helen Bateman
Senior Designer: Kylie Mulquin
Editorial Coordinators: Sarah Anderson, Tracey Gibson
Production Manager: Helen Creeke
Production Coordinator: Kylie Lawson
Business Manager: Emily Jahn
Vice President International Sales: Stuart Laurence

Project Editor: Susan Tomnay
Designer: Jacqueline Richards

A catalog record for this book is available from
the Library of Congress, Washington, DC.

ISBN 1 875137 61 0

Color reproduction by Colourscan Co Pte Ltd
Printed by Toppan Printing Co, (H.K.) Ltd
Printed in China

A Weldon Owen Production

CONTENTS

PART TWO

KINDS OF PASTA

Introduction

Pasta: a simple Italian word for a simple food that has appeared on Mediterranean and Asian tables for centuries. Yet pasta has become so popular with cooks everywhere in recent years that it has also come to mean a world of good eating in almost any language.

Why has pasta been elevated from ethnic favorite to international culinary superstar? Probably because it fits in so well with today's cooking style. People want food that is light, easily prepared, and superbly fresh, made with the season's best offerings. Pasta's subtle flavor and slightly chewy texture make it a perfect partner for fresh vegetables and herbs. And not only is pasta good to eat and quick to prepare, it also provides a healthy bonus: high-carbohydrate, low-fat pasta plays an important role in a well-balanced diet.

If long, thin spaghetti or tubular elbow macaroni are the pasta shapes that you are most familiar with, you are about to embark on a delicious voyage of discovery. The editors of *Pasta* have created over sixty new recipes that show off fresh and dried pasta in all its variety, including flavored pasta, and the wonderful packaged fresh pastas widely available in supermarkets and delicatessens.

In the pages to come you will be introduced to little bow ties known as farfalle, to pleated radiatori, to circular ruote with spokes like wagon wheels, to tight little twists called fusilli, and to many more, including new and tempting interpretations of classics like tortellini, ravioli, and lasagne. You will also learn how easy it is to make plain, wholewheat, spinach, tomato, and herb pasta in your own kitchen.

An introductory chapter covers the basics of preparing homemade pasta and the best way to cook your own or purchased pasta so that it is served properly al dente. Next is a collection of sauces infused with aromatic fresh herbs,

pungent garlic, and garden-picked vegetables that you will use again and again. Succeeding chapters explore the pleasures of particular types of pasta: ribbon, shaped, and stuffed pastas; layered pasta dishes; and hot and cold pasta salads. Every chapter is color-coded. Each recipe features a "steps-at-a-glance" box that uses these colors for quick reference to the photographic steps illustrating the techniques used in the recipe. Tips appear throughout, from basic equipment needs to helpful hints to a glossary of ingredients. From first step to last, every recipe is guaranteed to please.

U.S. cup measures are used throughout this book. Slight adjustments may need to be made to quantities if Imperial or Metric cups are used.

PART ONE

THE BASICS

A guide to one of the simplest of foods,
showing you how easy and satisfying
it is to make pasta at home, and six
recipes for sensational sauces
that should be in every pasta
cook's repertoire.

BASIC TOOLS FOR MAKING PASTA BY HAND

Making fresh pasta by hand requires mixing bowls and a wooden spoon plus a rolling pin to flatten the dough into paper-thin sheets and a knife to cut it into portions. To freeze the dough you will need a freezer-safe container.

mixing bowls

rolling pin

wooden spoon

chef's knife

freezer-safe container

Making Pasta by Hand

Making pasta is a little like culinary alchemy. With a minimum of mixing, kneading, and shaping, the simplest of ingredients — flour, water, oil, salt, and eggs — are transformed into edible gold. Homemade pasta is easy to prepare, whether by hand or with a simple pasta machine available at most kitchenware shops and department stores.

Why make your own pasta when you can purchase it ready-made? Because you can taste the difference. Homemade pasta is more tender and delicate than packaged pasta, and will fully absorb whatever sauce coats it. However, good-quality purchased fresh or dried pasta can be almost as satisfying as the pasta you prepare at home from scratch.

On the pages to come you'll learn to make delicate narrow and wide ribbons, wrappers for stuffing manicotti and cannelloni, the little bundles known as ravioli and tortellini, and broad sheets for layered lasagne. You'll also discover the secrets of hand-shaping bow tie–shaped farfalle, the little cups called orecchiette, and more. For all of these and for any dish in the book that requires homemade pasta, use the basic recipe on page 28. The recipe is so simple that after the first few times you prepare it you probably won't even need to refer to it, but for now you might want to put a marker on that page for quick reference. Or, use purchased fresh pasta, available in the refrigerated case of many supermarkets or delicatessens.

This section demonstrates the essential steps in making pasta dough completely by hand. The remainder of the chapter describes how to mix pasta dough with a food processor, and the proper way to knead and roll the dough with a hand-cranked pasta maker that clamps onto a kitchen bench or table. Succeeding chapters detail how to cut and shape pasta dough and how to identify and use the myriad dry pasta shapes available. Even the best pasta, whether fresh or dried, can be ruined if improperly cooked. The steps on pages 26 and 27 explain this elementary but critical technique. The recipes in this book require twice as much uncooked fresh pasta (homemade or purchased) as dried.

for herb pasta, add dried seasoning to flour mixture

for spinach pasta, add finely chopped cooked spinach to egg mixture

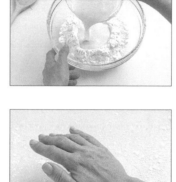

STEP 1

Adding Egg Mixture to Flour

Stir together flour and salt in a large mixing bowl. Make a well or depression in the center. In another bowl combine eggs, water, and oil and pour liquid into the well. Mix thoroughly with a wooden spoon.

knead until dough is smooth and elastic (8 to 10 minutes)

STEP 2

Kneading by Hand

Turn out the dough onto a lightly floured work surface. To knead, curve your fingers over the edge of the dough and pull it toward you. Then push down and away with the heel of your hand. Give the dough a quarter turn, fold toward you, and repeat the process. Cover and let rest for 10 minutes before rolling out.

The Basics

if the dough shrinks back while rolling, let it rest several minutes under a kitchen towel or sheet of plastic wrap, then continue

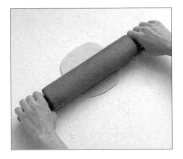

STEP 3

Rolling the Dough

Divide the dough into recipe-sized portions, usually in quarters. Set one portion on a floured work surface. Flatten with a rolling pin to about ⅛ in/3 mm thickness. Cover the remaining dough with a kitchen towel or plastic wrap so it won't dry out, or freeze for later use as shown on page 17.

the surface of rolled-out dough must dry somewhat or it will stick together when cut

STEP 4

Rolling Dough to ¹⁄₁₆ in/2 mm

Continue rolling the dough until it is ¹⁄₁₆ in/2 mm thick. A one-quarter portion will roll out to a square that is about 12x12 in/30x30 cm. After rolling, let the dough rest, uncovered, for 20 minutes to allow the surface to dry slightly.

STORING DOUGH

after cutting,
shape each
quarter portion
into a ball and
then flatten

STEP 1

Dividing the Dough

After kneading, shape the dough into a round;
do not roll out. Divide the round into quarters or
whatever portion size is specified in the recipe,
using a sharp knife.

to use, thaw
several hours in
the refrigerator
or about 1 hour
at room
temperature

STEP 2

Freezing Dough

Wrap each portion airtight in plastic wrap.
Then store in a freezer-safe container or in heavy-duty
freezer bags. The dough will keep in the freezer
for up to 8 months.

Making Pasta by Machine

When pasta dough is mixed in a food processor, then rolled out to paper thinness in a manual pasta maker, the whole process becomes very fast and almost effortless.

As usual, the food processor does its job quickly. Carefully watch the dough at every step. If you don't have a pasta machine, you can knead food processor dough with your hands and roll it out with a rolling pin as shown in steps 2, 3, and 4 on pages 15 and 16. However, the hand-turned pasta machine is inexpensive compared to most home appliances and small enough to store out of sight when not in use. If you make pasta often, it might be a sensible purchase because it takes most of the work out of kneading and rolling the dough.

Start at the lowest setting, with the rollers wide apart; usually two passes through each setting will be enough. If the sheet of dough feeds through the rollers easily and looks smooth and silky, almost rubbery, without rough spots, turn to the next setting. If you have to crank hard, go back to a wider setting. Continue until the dough is the proper texture and thickness, usually $1/16$ in/2 mm thick.

BASIC TOOLS FOR MAKING PASTA BY MACHINE

To prepare pasta by machine, use a small bowl, a measuring cup, a rubber spatula, and a food processor to mix the ingredients, and a hand-cranked pasta maker to knead and roll the dough.

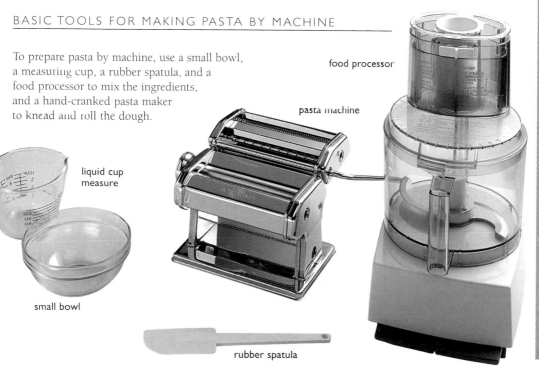

food processor

pasta machine

liquid cup measure

small bowl

rubber spatula

add chopped cooked spinach during this step if making spinach pasta by machine

stir the liquid ingredients together with a fork before pouring so they will blend more smoothly

if you let the dough rest after processing, it will be easier to roll out

STEP 1

Processing Flour and Eggs

Place flour, salt, and eggs in the work bowl of a food processor. Cover and process with a pulsing action until the mixture is the consistency of fine crumbs. This happens very quickly, so be careful that you don't overprocess.

STEP 2

Adding Liquid

Put water, oil, and any other liquid in a measuring cup with a lip. With the processor running, slowly pour the liquid through the feed tube into the work bowl. The flour mixture will begin to form a cohesive mass.

STEP 3

Forming a Ball

Continue processing the mixture only until the dough forms a ball. Stop once or twice to scrape down the sides of the work bowl so all the ingredients are incorporated into the dough. Remove from the work bowl, cover, and let rest 10 minutes.

sprinkle dough lightly with flour before each pass through the machine so it doesn't stick

STEP 4

Kneading in Pasta Machine

Divide the dough into 4 portions or as directed in the recipe. Cover unused dough or freeze (see page 17). Flatten one portion and feed through the rollers at the widest setting. Fold in half or thirds, give a quarter turn, and run through the same setting. Repeat until the dough is smooth and no longer tears.

when done, let dough sheet rest for 20 minutes on a lightly floured towel before shaping

if dough becomes too long to handle, cut it in half

STEP 5

Rolling in Pasta Machine

Turn to the next narrow setting. Lightly flour the dough, fold, give a quarter turn, and pass through the machine again. Repeat folding, turning, and rolling at increasingly higher (narrower) settings until the dough is $1/16$ in/2 mm thick.

Cooking Pasta

Always use a large pot so pasta can circulate freely in vigorously boiling water with room to expand as it cooks. If the pot is too small, the pasta will stick together; you also risk an overflow of the scalding, bubbling liquid. A pasta pot with a strainer insert is practical: it lets you drain off the water with very little effort because the water flows back into the pot when you lift the insert. Salt may be added to the water for flavor (bring the water back to the boil after adding), and oil helps keep pasta from sticking, but neither is a must.

Fresh pasta never needs more than a few minutes to cook. Dried ribbons and shapes take longer; times vary from 8 to 15 minutes (check the package for recommended cooking times). Both types are done when the texture is tender but still slightly chewy and no traces of raw pasta remain when you bite into a piece — a quality described as "al dente". Drain, then transfer to a warm serving bowl and toss immediately with sauce or use as directed in the recipe. A wooden or plastic pasta rake works best for tossing and serving pasta strands.

BASIC TOOLS FOR COOKING PASTA

A large pasta pot lets pasta tumble freely in the bubbling water. The cooking liquid drains away afterwards through a strainer insert. Or use a free-standing colander. Use a pasta rake for tossing and serving long strands.

colander

pasta pot

wooden pasta rake

plastic pasta rake

Useful Information for Cooking Pasta

**Here are a few simple guidelines for cooking pasta.
The two main rules are: use the best pasta available and don't overcook it.**

Always take note of the cooking directions on the packets of commercial pasta. Cooking times vary from brand to brand.

• Dried pasta needs about 10 minutes cooking time – start testing it after 8 minutes. Freshly made pasta, however, is much faster. It should be ready within 1½ to 2 minutes, but start testing it after 1 minute. Cooking times vary according to the thickness and shape of the pasta. The only successful way to test pasta is to taste it.

• When purchasing pasta, always choose the best quality available, whether it be dried or fresh. The best pasta is made from hard durum wheat. High-quality dried pasta (usually imported from Italy) is characterized by a dull finish and tiny abrasions on the surface. These abrasions trap and hold the sauce. Smooth, shiny, commercial pasta, which is made in great quantities and dried at high temperatures, doesn't have the flavor of these slowly dried artisan-made pastas, but it is cheaper.

• Pasta should never be overcooked. "Al dente" is a term used to describe perfectly cooked pasta – just tender and still a little resistant.

• A tall, large capacity saucepan is essential for cooking pasta to ensure there is sufficient water. The approximate ratio of dry pasta to boiling water is 4 to 8 oz (125 to 250 g) to 12 cups/3 qt/3 l. Add a further quart/liter of water for each additional 8 oz/250g pasta. If you want to add salt, bring the water to the boil, add salt (allow 1 teaspoon of salt to 12 cups/3 qt/3 l of water), bring the water back to the boil and then add the pasta.

• Oil can be added to the boiling water to prevent the pasta strands from sticking together, but if you've used enough water in a large enough pan, it shouldn't be necessary.

• The moment the pasta is cooked it should be transferred to a warm serving dish or bowl.

If it is not coated with sauce immediately, but left to stand, the strands will stick together and become unpleasantly gummy.

• There should be enough sauce to coat the pasta thoroughly but not so much that it takes over. The pasta should always remain dominant in the dish.

For best flavor and texture, drain pasta thoroughly so no cooking water sticks to the pieces and dilutes the sauce.

for long strands, like spaghetti, dip one end of the batch in water until softened, then curl it around pan and lower it into the water

STEP 1

Adding Pasta to Water
Fill a large pot with 12 cups/3 qt/3 l of water (for 4 to 8 oz/125 to 250 g of pasta). Bring to a vigorous, rolling boil. Add 1 teaspoon of salt and 1 tablespoon of oil, if desired. Then add the pasta, a little at a time, so the water stays at the boil.

adjust the heat, if necessary, to keep the water boiling

STEP 2

Stirring Occasionally
Stir occasionally with a wooden spoon or pasta rake to keep the strands or pieces from sticking together as they swirl around in the water.

the Italians say pasta is done when it is *al dente,* or "to the tooth"

STEP 3

Testing for Doneness
Near the end of cooking time, taste often to check for doneness. Pasta is ready when the texture is tender, but still slightly firm, or "al dente." Don't let the pasta sit in the cooking water or it will overcook and get mushy.

TWO WAYS TO DRAIN

give the insert a
few shakes to
remove any
remaining water
from the pasta

STEP 1

Removing Drainer Insert

If using a pasta pot with an insert, lift up the insert by
the handles (protect your hands with oven pads, if
necessary). Hold it above the water for a few seconds;
the cooking water will drain back into the pot.

using a fork or a
pasta rake, stir the
pasta once or
twice to ensure
all the water
runs out

STEP 2

Draining in a Colander

Stand a colander in the sink. If using a standard pot
without a drainer insert, pour the pasta and water
into the colander as soon as the pasta is done.

Homemade Pasta

This simple dough can be used for every recipe in this book that requires fresh pasta. Although quick to prepare, to save more time you can make the dough ahead and freeze it (see the tip box on page 17 for freezing and thawing directions). To substitute fresh pasta in a recipe that specifies dried, use 8 oz/250 g fresh for every 4 oz/125 g of dried pasta.

INGREDIENTS

2 cups/8 oz/250 g all-purpose (plain) flour

$^1/_2$ teaspoon salt

2 beaten eggs

$^1/_3$ cup/3 fl oz/80 ml water

1 teaspoon olive oil or cooking oil

$^1/_3$ cup/1$^1/_2$ oz/45 g all-purpose (plain) flour for sprinkling

Preparation Time 1$^1/_4$ hours
Makes four 4-oz/125-g portions of pasta (1 lb/500 g total)

STEPS AT A GLANCE	Page
■ Making pasta	12–31

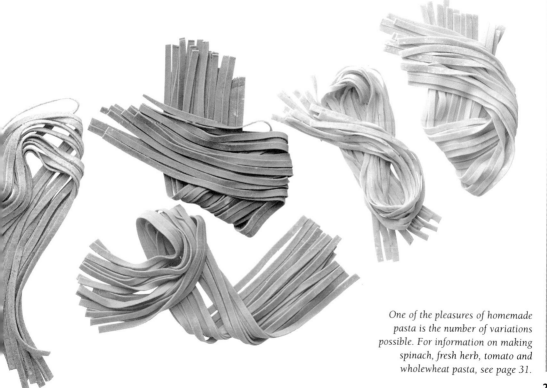

One of the pleasures of homemade pasta is the number of variations possible. For information on making spinach, fresh herb, tomato and wholewheat pasta, see page 31.

METHOD FOR MAKING HOMEMADE PASTA

In a large mixing bowl stir together the 2 cups/ 8 oz/250 g flour and salt. Make a well in center.

In a small mixing bowl stir together the eggs, water, and olive oil or cooking oil. Add to the flour mixture and mix well.

Sprinkle kneading surface with the ⅓ cup/ 1½ oz/45 g flour. (Spinach, wholewheat, and tomato variations may not require the addition of any or all of this flour.) Turn dough out onto floured surface. Knead till dough is smooth and elastic (8 to 10 minutes total). Cover and let rest for 10 minutes.

Divide dough into quarters. On a lightly floured surface, roll each quarter into a 12-in/30-cm square about ¹⁄₁₆ in/2 mm thick. Let stand for about 20 minutes, or till slightly dry. Or, if using a pasta machine, pass each quarter of dough through machine, according to manufacturer's directions, till ¹⁄₁₆ in/2 mm thick. Shape or stuff as desired, or as directed in recipe.

To dry ribbons, hang pasta from a pasta-drying rack or clothes hanger, or toss with flour, shape into loose bundles, and place on a floured baking sheet. Let dry overnight or till completely dry. Place in an airtight container and refrigerate for up to 3 days. Or, dry the pasta for at least 1 hour, seal it in a freezer bag or container, and freeze for up to 8 months.

Per portion plain pasta 292 calories/1,226 kilojoules, 10 g protein, 51 g carbohydrate, 4 g total fat (1 g saturated), 107 mg cholesterol, 300 mg sodium, 102 mg potassium

FRESH PASTA VARIATIONS

Wholewheat pasta
Prepare pasta as directed, except substitute wholewheat flour for all-purpose (plain) flour. You may need to use a little more liquid.

Fresh herb pasta
A single herb or mixture of herbs can be used. The herbs must be washed, dried, and finely chopped. Add ½ cup (½ oz/15 g) of fresh herbs to flour and proceed as for plain pasta dough.

Spinach pasta
Prepare as directed, except decrease the water to 3 tablespoons and add 2½ oz/75g very finely chopped cooked spinach, well drained, to the egg mixture.

Tomato pasta
Prepare pasta as directed, except substitute tomato paste for the water.

BASIC SAUCES

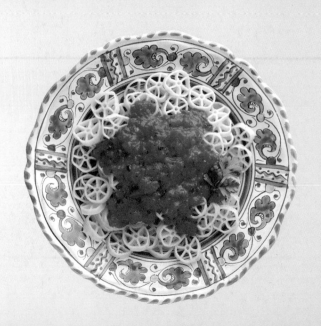

Preparing Sauce Ingredients

Favorite sauces for pasta range from the simplicity of garlic-infused olive oil or melted butter — for which no recipe is needed — to herbal pestos and rich, complex concoctions of cream, cheese, and eggs. Tomatoes and pasta are a classic pairing with endless uses. In this chapter, you'll find a selection of basic sauces that can be served over your favorite hot cooked pasta or used as directed in other recipes in this book.

As with all dishes, a pasta sauce is only as good as what you put into it. For red sauces, fully ripened fresh plum (Roma) tomatoes are best. They are meaty and juicy, not watery,

and cook down into a thicker mixture. If they aren't available, canned plum tomatoes (also sometimes labelled "Italian-style tomatoes") are preferable to fresh ones that are unripe or flavorless. Fresh herbs, whether basil, parsley, or oregano, should look lively, not wilted, while dried herbs should be less than 6 months old and have a characteristic aroma. Finally, there is no comparison between freshly grated Parmesan or other hard cheese, hand-grated from a wedge, and packaged grated cheese. Resist the temptation to use pre-grated cheeses and you'll find your sauces taste even better than you expected.

BASIC TOOLS FOR PREPARING SAUCE INGREDIENTS

Use sharp knives and kitchen scissors to peel, slice, or chop vegetables and snip leafy herbs. Special tools include a press for mincing garlic and a grater with fine holes for Parmesan. A colander, bowl, and measuring cup hold ingredients.

colander

small bowl

cutting board, Parmesan grater, and garlic press

measuring cup

scissors

small, sharp knife

chef's knife

in the boiling water, the tomato skin will split at the X and peel away easily

STEP 1

Peeling Tomatoes

Cut an X in the blossom end of the tomato with the point of a knife, then plunge the tomato into boiling water for 20 to 30 seconds to loosen the skin. Transfer to a colander to drain. When cool enough to handle, peel off the skin by pulling it away with a small, sharp knife.

stubborn seeds can also be coaxed out with a knife or your finger

STEP 2

Seeding Tomatoes

Cut the peeled tomato in half crosswise with a sharp knife. Hold the cut half upside down over the sink and squeeze gently to force out most of the seeds.

if the recipe calls for drained tomatoes, pour into a sieve, then cut up

STEP 3

Cutting Up Canned Tomatoes

Insert a pair of sharp kitchen scissors with long blades into the can of whole tomatoes (no need to drain off the juice). Open and close the blades to cut the tomatoes into small pieces. Or, pour tomatoes into a bowl and then cut up.

to grate a large amount of Parmesan cheese, drop chunks into a running food processor fitted with a metal blade

STEP 4

Grating Fresh Parmesan

Rub a chunk of fresh Parmesan cheese across the holes of a hand grater. If you grate fresh cheese often, you may want to purchase a hand-turned winder-style grater that you can bring to the table.

you can also chop
delicate herbs
with a knife, but
snipping with
scissors is gentler
and there is less
chance of mashing
the leaves

STEP 5

Chopping Fresh Herbs

Strip the leaves of fresh herbs from their stems. Discard
the stems and place the leaves in a measuring cup or
bowl. Snip into small pieces with kitchen scissors.

you can also
mince garlic with
a knife

STEP 6

Mincing Garlic

Remove a clove of garlic from the head. Peel away the
papery skin unless your garlic press will mince cloves
with the skin intact. Squeeze the arms of the press
together to force the garlic through the holes into a bowl.

grip the onion half with your fingers to keep it steady

STEP 7

Chopping Onions

Halve the onion lengthwise and peel, leaving the onion attached to the root end. Place one half, cut-side down, on a work surface. With a sharp knife, make a series of vertical cuts almost to the root end. Then make a series of evenly spaced horizontal cuts and discard the root end.

you may want to reserve some sauce to pass at the table

STEP 8

Tossing Pasta

Use a large bowl to allow plenty of room for tossing. Warm the bowl first to keep the pasta hot. Add about half of the sauce to the pasta; toss to coat the strands, then add the remaining sauce and toss again.

All pasta cooks should have a basic tomato sauce in their repertoire and a supply of ready-made in the freezer to use at a moment's notice.

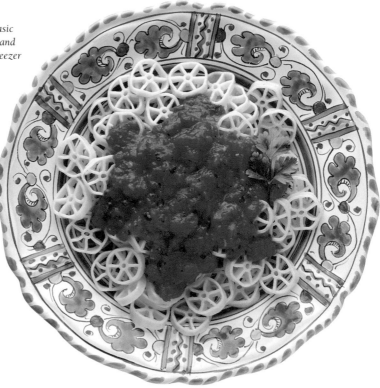

Classic Tomato Sauce

If you like your tomato sauce chunky, skip the blending or processing step and serve it hot from the pan. If you like, add meatballs to the sauce (see recipe, page 116).

INGREDIENTS

4 lb/2 kg ripe plum (Roma) tomatoes or 45 oz/1.3 kg canned whole Italian-style tomatoes, with juice

2 tablespoons olive oil or cooking oil

2 cloves garlic, minced

1/2 teaspoon salt

1/2 teaspoon sugar

1/4 teaspoon pepper

1/3 cup/1 oz/30 g chopped fresh basil, oregano, or parsley

Preparation Time 40 minutes
Cooking Time 25 minutes
Makes about 4 cups/32 fl oz/1 liter

STEPS AT A GLANCE   Page

Peel, seed, and finely chop the fresh plum tomatoes, if using. In a large saucepan or Dutch oven, heat olive oil or cooking oil over medium heat. Add fresh or undrained canned tomatoes, garlic, salt (omit if using canned tomatoes), sugar, and pepper. Bring to boiling; reduce heat. Simmer, uncovered, for about 20 minutes, or to desired consistency. Place about half the sauce in a food processor bowl or blender container; process or blend till smooth. Return blended tomato mixture to saucepan. Stir in basil, oregano, or parsley. Cook for 5 minutes more.

Per 1 cup/8 fl oz/250 ml 160 calories/672 kilojoules, 4 g protein, 22 g carbohydrate, 8 g total fat (1 g saturated), 0 mg cholesterol, 308 mg sodium, 1,030 mg potassium

STEP 1

Simmering Sauce

To achieve the desired consistency, bring the sauce ingredients to a boil, then reduce the heat and simmer uncovered, stirring now and then. This allows the excess liquid to evaporate and the flavors to become concentrated. When the tomatoes are broken down and the sauce is no longer runny, the sauce is done.

STEP 2

Blending Sauce

Purée about half of the sauce in a blender or food processor. Return to the saucepan; add chopped herbs (fresh herbs are added at the last minute to preserve their fresh flavor). Cook 5 minutes more.

Bolognese Sauce

Experiment with substituting Italian-style sausage or smoked sausage for the beef, or use a combination of veal and pork, which is the mark of a traditional Bolognese sauce.

INGREDIENTS

2 lb/1 kg ripe plum (Roma) tomatoes or 30 oz/940 g canned whole Italian-style tomatoes, drained

12 oz/375 g lean ground (minced) beef

5 oz/155 g finely chopped onion

2½ oz/75 g finely chopped carrot

2½ oz/75 g finely chopped celery

2 slices bacon, finely chopped

½ cup/4 fl oz/125 ml dry red wine

¾ cup/6 fl oz/180 ml heavy (double) cream

½ teaspoon salt

¼ teaspoon pepper

⅛ teaspoon ground nutmeg

Preparation Time 30 minutes
Cooking Time 38 to 40 minutes
Makes 4 cups/32 fl oz/1 liter

The ancient city of Bologna, Italy, gave its name to a tasty meat sauce that makes a hearty meal when combined with any pasta shape. Italians also call the sauce "ragu".

METHOD FOR MAKING BOLOGNESE SAUCE

Peel and seed fresh plum tomatoes, if using. In a food processor bowl or blender container process or blend fresh or canned tomatoes till smooth; set aside.

In a large frying pan cook ground beef, onion, carrot, celery, and bacon for 5 minutes, or till meat is brown and vegetables are tender, stirring to break the meat into tiny pieces. Drain off fat. Add the wine. Bring to boiling; reduce heat. Simmer, uncovered, for 3 to 5 minutes, or till nearly all of the liquid has evaporated, stirring occasionally.

Stir in tomatoes. Cover and simmer for 30 minutes, or to desired consistency, stirring occasionally. Stir in cream, salt (omit if using canned tomatoes), pepper, and nutmeg. Heat through.

Per 1 cup/8 fl oz/250 ml 436 calories/1,831 kilojoules, 21 g protein, 22 g carbohydrate, 29 g total fat (15 g saturated), 117 mg cholesterol, 428 mg sodium, 1,069 mg potassium

STEP 1

Grating Nutmeg

Rub a whole nutmeg across the grating holes of a nutmeg grater. Work over a piece of waxed paper or a bowl to collect the grated spice. Packaged ground nutmeg is an acceptable substitute for fresh, but it won't be as aromatic or flavorsome.

STEP 2

Browning Meat

Cook the meat until it is brown and the vegetables are tender, stirring with a wooden spoon to break the ground meat into little pieces.

STEP 3

Adding Cream

Cream is added last to thicken and enrich the sauce. Pour it in while stirring to keep the cream from boiling over. Stir to blend thoroughly and cook a few minutes more to heat through.

Smooth, fragrant pesto coats strands of pasta with the incomparable flavor of fresh-picked basil.

Pesto

A little pesto has a lot of flavor, so for a simple accompaniment for two to three people, use about ¼ cup/2 fl oz/60 ml of pesto tossed with 4 oz/125 g dried or 8 oz/250 g fresh pasta, cooked and drained.

INGREDIENTS

1½ cups/1½ oz/45 g firmly packed fresh basil leaves

¼ cup/1 oz/30 g grated Parmesan cheese

¼ cup/1 oz/30 g grated Romano cheese

¼ cup/1½ oz/45 g pine nuts or flaked almonds

1 large clove garlic, sliced

⅛ teaspoon salt

¼ cup/2 fl oz/60 ml olive oil or cooking oil

Preparation Time 15 minutes
Makes ¾ cup/6 fl oz/180 ml

STEPS AT A GLANCE	Page
Grating fresh Parmesan	37

In a food processor bowl or blender container combine basil, Parmesan cheese, Romano cheese, pine nuts or almonds, garlic, and salt. Pour in olive oil or cooking oil. Cover and process or blend with several on/off turns till a purée forms, stopping the machine several times and cleaning the sides with a rubber spatula. Add to hot pasta as directed in recipes.

Store any remaining pesto in ¼ cup/2-fl oz/60-ml portions, wrapped and frozen for up to 1 year or refrigerated for up to 2 days. Before using, bring to room temperature.

Per tablespoon 98 calories/411 kilojoules, 3 g protein, 1 g carbohydrate, 8 g total fat (2 g saturated), 4 mg cholesterol, 89 mg sodium, 74 mg potassium

STEP 1

Adding Ingredients
Pour oil over the other pesto ingredients. The work bowl of the food processor should be fitted with the metal blade.

STEP 2

Finishing Sauce
Process with a few on/off pulses until a purée forms. Scrape down the sides of the work bowl a few times between pulses to blend.

STEP 3

Storing Sauce
Spoon ¼-cup/2-fl oz/60-ml portions into small freezer containers. Before securing the lid, cover the pesto surface with plastic wrap to prevent browning. The frozen sauce will keep for up to 1 year.

Tomato-Vegetable Sauce

This traditional Italian sauce is never made with meat. Spoon it over hot cooked pasta and sprinkle with a little feta cheese or Parmesan cheese for a scrumptious vegetarian dish.

INGREDIENTS

8 oz/250 g fresh mushrooms, thinly sliced

2¹/₂ oz/75 g chopped onion

2 cloves garlic, minced

1 tablespoon olive oil or cooking oil

2 cups/10 oz/315 g shredded zucchini (courgettes)

15 oz/470 g canned Italian-style chunky tomato sauce

¹/₂ cup/4 fl oz/125 ml dry red wine

1 tablespoon chopped fresh sage

¹/₄ teaspoon salt

¹/₄ teaspoon pepper

Preparation Time 20 minutes
Cooking Time 20 to 25 minutes
Makes 4 cups/32 fl oz/1 liter

STEPS AT A GLANCE   Page

This sauce is chunkier and more complex than a simple tomato sauce. Red wine adds body, and sliced mushrooms and shredded zucchini lend texture and depth of flavor.

In a large frying pan cook mushrooms, onion, and garlic in hot olive oil or cooking oil for 5 minutes, stirring constantly. Add zucchini and cook for 5 minutes, or till vegetables are tender but not brown. Add tomato sauce, wine, sage, salt, and pepper. Bring to boiling; reduce heat. Simmer, uncovered, for 10 to 15 minutes, or to desired consistency, stirring frequently.

Per 1 cup/8 fl oz/250 ml 115 calories/483 kilojoules, 3 g protein, 15 g carbohydrate, 4 g total fat (1 g saturated), 0 mg cholesterol, 798 mg sodium, 785 mg potassium

Hearty Sausage & Tomato Sauce

Adjust the level of heat to your liking by selecting either plain or hot Italian
sausage meat. Besides serving this sauce over pasta, you could also
use it as a base for a hot and spicy chili sauce.

INGREDIENTS

2 lb/1 kg ripe plum (Roma)
tomatoes or 30 oz/940 g canned
Italian-style tomatoes, cut up,
drained

12 oz/375 g Italian-style sausage
meat (casings removed)

2½ oz/75 g chopped onion

2 oz/60 g finely chopped green
pepper (capsicum)

2 cloves garlic, minced

¾ cup/6 oz/185 g tomato paste

½ teaspoon salt

½ teaspoon dried oregano,
crushed

½ teaspoon dried basil,
crushed

¼ teaspoon ground
red pepper (cayenne)

Preparation Time 30 minutes
Cooking Time 45 to 50 minutes
Makes 4 cups/32 fl oz/1 liter

METHOD FOR MAKING HEARTY SAUSAGE & TOMATO SAUCE

Peel, seed, and chop the fresh plum tomatoes, if using.

In a large saucepan cook the Italian sausage, onion, green pepper, and garlic for 5 minutes, or till sausage is brown. Drain off fat. Carefully stir in the fresh or undrained canned tomatoes, tomato paste, salt, oregano, basil, and red pepper. Bring to boiling; reduce heat. Cover and simmer for 30 minutes. Then uncover and simmer for 10 to 15 minutes more, or until it reaches the desired consistency, stirring occasionally.

Per 1 cup/8 fl oz/250 ml 313 calories/1,314 kilojoules, 17 g protein, 25 g carbohydrate, 17 g total fat (6 g saturated), 49 mg cholesterol, 898 mg sodium, 1,274 mg potassium

STEPS AT A GLANCE   Page

▨ Preparing sauce ingredients **34**
▨ Simmering sauce   **43**

*Combine this robust meat sauce
with an equally substantial
pasta such as penne.*

Creamy Parmesan Sauce

Combine this rich cheese sauce with pasta ribbons and you have the classic pasta dish, fettuccine Alfredo. As the sauce is poured over the cooked pasta, the heat cooks the sauce, causing the cream to thicken slightly and the cheese to melt.

Fresh tomato pasta provides a subtle contrast to this rich and creamy cheese sauce. Serve with a favorite grilled chop and fresh vegetable.

INGREDIENTS

1/3 cup/3 fl oz/80 ml light (single) or heavy (double) cream

2 tablespoons margarine or butter

4 oz/125 g dried or 8 oz/250 g fresh tomato, herb, or plain fettuccine

1/3 cup/1 1/2 oz/45 g grated Parmesan cheese

1/4 teaspoon salt

1 small clove garlic, minced

1 tablespoon chopped fresh basil or fresh parsley (optional)

coarsely ground black pepper (optional)

Preparation Time 50 minutes (includes warming cream & butter)
Cooking Time 2 to 10 minutes
Serves 4 as an accompaniment or 2 as a main course

Allow cream and margarine or butter to come to room temperature (about 40 minutes).

In a large saucepan or pasta pot bring 12 cups/3 qt/3 l water to boiling. Add pasta. Reduce heat slightly. Boil, uncovered, for 8 to 10 minutes for dried pasta or 1 1/2 to 2 minutes for fresh pasta, or till al dente, stirring occasionally. (Or, cook according to package directions.) Immediately drain.

Return pasta to the warm pan. Add Parmesan cheese, cream, margarine or butter, salt, and garlic. Toss gently till pasta is well coated. Transfer to a warm serving dish. If desired, sprinkle with basil or parsley and pepper. Serve immediately.

Per serving 282 calories/1,184 kilojoules, 10 g protein, 35 g carbohydrate, 11 g total fat (4 g saturated), 13 mg cholesterol, 363 mg sodium, 78 mg potassium

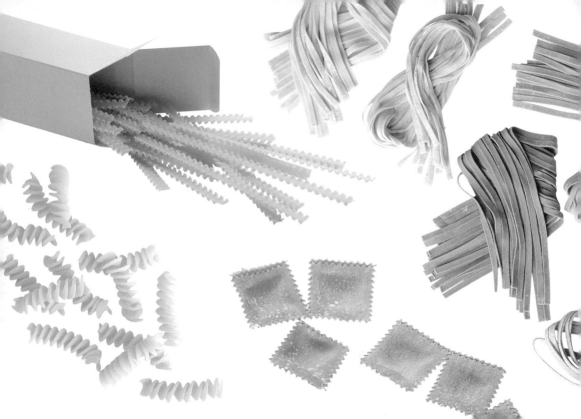

PART TWO

KINDS OF PASTA

Recipes and information on all the different ways
to prepare pasta are featured here: pasta that's
cut into ribbons, formed into shapes,
layered with other ingredients,
stuffed, and made
into salads.

RIBBON PASTA

BASIC TOOLS FOR MAKING RIBBON PASTA

Cut sheets of fresh pasta into ribbons with a small, sharp knife or with a pasta machine. To dry, drape the noodles over the rods of a pasta drying rack or arrange them on a baking sheet.

pasta drying rack

cutting board and baking sheet

pasta machine

small, sharp knife

Cutting Ribbon Pasta

Among the most versatile of all pastas are the silky, flat ribbons cut from fresh dough. They are also the simplest of shapes to form. Called by a variety of names, depending on the width of the noodle, all ribbon pastas are superb with creamy sauces, pesto, and tomato-based sauces.

Homemade pasta ribbons with straight edges can be cut with a sharp knife or with the roller blades of a pasta machine (only a commercial machine will produce ribbons with ruffled edges). The cutting blades of a hand-turned pasta machine are preset to two prescribed sizes: 1/4 in/6 mm wide for fettuccine or 1/16 in/2 mm wide for fine noodles – a similar size to spaghetti. When you cut the dough with a knife, the strips can be the traditional widths or any that appeal to you, including wide lasagne sheets (see page 202).

After you have made the dough and rolled it out (see pages 16 and 21), it must rest on a towel, uncovered, for about 20 minutes to allow the surface to dry slightly. This step keeps the pasta from sticking when it is rolled and sliced with a knife or when it is fed through the machine. If the sheets are very long, cut them into a manageable length.

CUTTING RIBBON PASTA

The steps on pages 67 to 69 show how to create ribbons by cutting a sheet of rolled dough with a knife or with a hand-turned pasta machine. After you have cut the ribbons by either method, the pasta can dry for up to 1 hour before it is cooked. You can drape it over the dowels of a special wooden pasta rack, or wrap it into little nests and place in a lightly floured baking sheet. If the pasta will not be used immediately, let it dry completely, preferably overnight. Once dried, place it in an airtight container and store in the refrigerator for up to 3 days. To freeze for up to 8 months, let the ribbons dry for 1 hour, then seal in a freezer bag or container.

Homemade pasta that has been fully dried can be used interchangeably with packaged dried pasta in the recipes in this book. If cooking homemade ribbons right away, follow the directions given for fresh pasta.

rolling the dough into a tube makes it easier to slice into uniform ribbons

STEP 1

Rolling Up Dough

After the surface of the thin dough sheet has dried slightly, roll up the sheet loosely like a jelly roll. Don't squeeze the roll or the dough might stick together.

if your knife is dull it will compress the roll rather than slice it cleanly

STEP 2

Cutting Dough

Be sure your knife is very sharp. Slice the rolled dough into 1/4-in/6-mm-wide strips for fettuccine, 1/8-in/3-mm-wide strips for linguine, or any width desired. For lasagne, cut the dough into 2 1/2-in/6-cm-wide strips or wider sheets.

turn the handle
clockwise only or
the sheets won't
pass through
the blades

STEP 3

Machine-cutting Fettuccine

Secure the cutting attachment to the machine.
If necessary, cut the rolled pasta sheet in half to match
the width of the machine. Feed the pasta sheet through
the 1/4-in/6-mm-wide cutters.

to make ribbons
of the same
length, be sure the
sheet is fed
through evenly

STEP 4

Machine-cutting Fine Strands

To make narrower strands, simply feed the rolled pasta
sheet through the fine cutters, rather than the wider
fettuccine blades. The fine strands will be more delicate
than fettuccine, so handle them carefully. Use as you
would spaghetti.

DRYING PASTA

separate the
strands so they
won't stick
together

STEP 1

Rack Drying

Loosely gather the ribbons and hang them on the dowels of a pasta drying rack. 1 lb/500 g of ribbons should fit on most standard racks.

use a metal
baking sheet or a
jelly roll pan

STEP 2

Drying on a Baking Sheet

Toss the pasta ribbons in flour and loosely shape into bundles. Arrange in a flour-dusted baking sheet to dry.

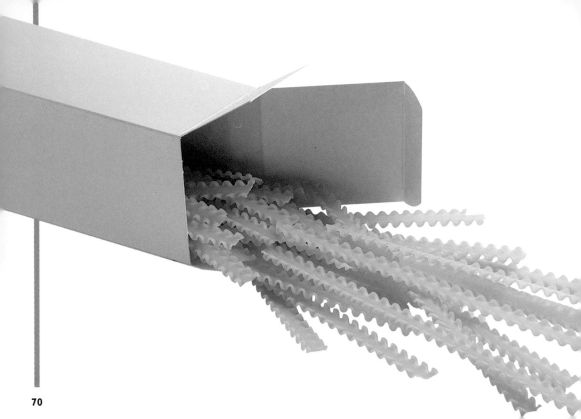

Dried Pasta Ribbons and Strands

In the complicated hierarchy of Italian ribbon-pasta nomenclature, almost infinitesimal differences in width result in a different pasta. Names can also differ from one part of Italy to the other (for example, 1/4-in/6-mm-wide ribbons are called fettuccine in most regions, except in parts of the north where they are called tagliatelle), or from manufacturer to manufacturer. If a recipe requires a particular ribbon and you can't find it in the shop, be assured that you will come across another that is very similar to the one you need and that will work just as well. The best dried pasta is made from semolina flour or durum flour, both ground from hard durum wheat. Unlike fresh ribbon pasta, dried ribbon pasta may take the form of long, narrow rods (spaghetti and vermicelli), twisted strands (fusilli), or ruffled ribbons (mafalde).

Ribbon pastas also appear throughout Asia. While dried Italian pasta is made with flour, water, and sometimes egg, Asian noodles use wheat, buckwheat, and rice flours, or vegetable starches made from beans or potatoes. Some incorporate egg, while others don't. Packaged Asian pastas are available at Asian groceries and some supermarkets.

Ribbon Pasta

Here's a look at some of the most widely available dried pasta ribbons and strands. Although similar, each is different enough to add its own unique character to a dish. Buckwheat noodles (soba) are used in Asian dishes.

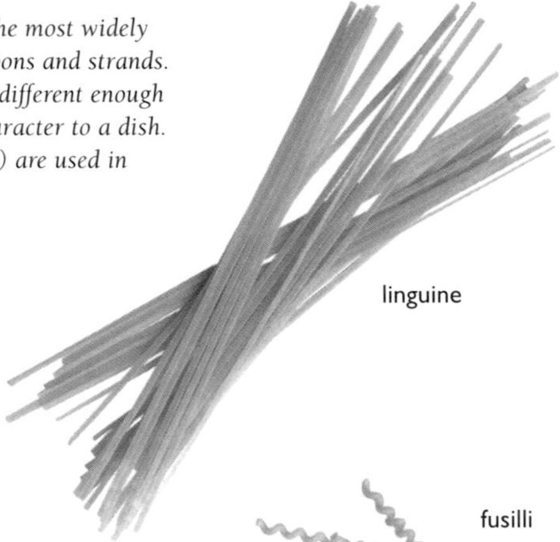

linguine

fettuccine

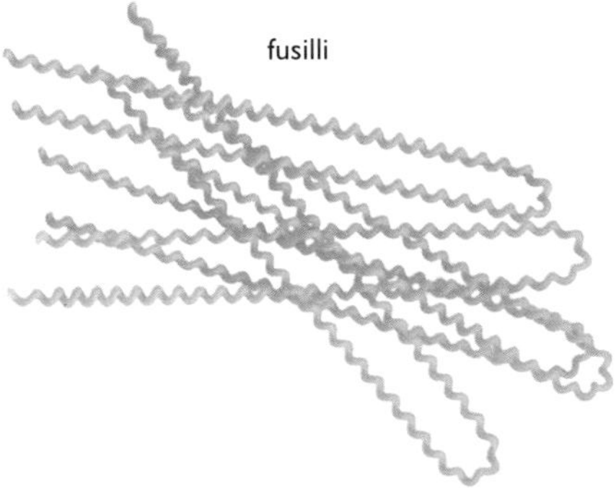

fusilli

capellini
or angel hair

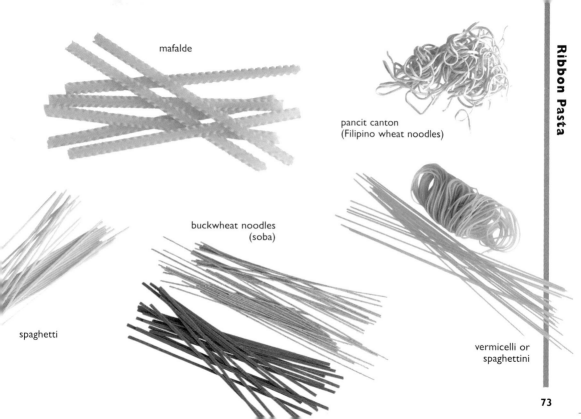

mafalde

pancit canton
(Filipino wheat noodles)

buckwheat noodles
(soba)

spaghetti

vermicelli or
spaghettini

Pancetta (Italian bacon) seasons this tangy sauce brightened with greens and baby squash or zucchini.

Fettuccine with Sweet & Sour Vegetables

If you decide to use spinach or Swiss chard (silverbeet) instead of kale, take note that they cook in much less time. Start by cooking the pasta, then cook the vegetables.

INGREDIENTS

6 oz/180 g kale, spinach, or Swiss chard (silverbeet)

6 oz/180 g yellow baby squash or zucchini (courgettes), cut into 1/4-in/6-mm-thick slices

4 oz/125 g dried fettuccine or linguine or 8 oz/250 g fresh fettuccine or linguine

1 oz/30 g pancetta or thick-sliced bacon, finely chopped

2 tablespoons olive oil or cooking oil

2 oz/60 g chopped onion

1 tablespoon all-purpose (plain) flour

1 tablespoon sugar

1/2 teaspoon salt

1/8 teaspoon pepper

3/4 cup/6 fl oz/180 ml chicken stock

1/4 cup/2 fl oz/60 ml red wine vinegar

Preparation Time 20 minutes
Cooking Time 28 to 30 minutes
Serves 4 as an accompaniment or first course

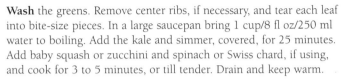

Wash the greens. Remove center ribs, if necessary, and tear each leaf into bite-size pieces. In a large saucepan bring 1 cup/8 fl oz/250 ml water to boiling. Add the kale and simmer, covered, for 25 minutes. Add baby squash or zucchini and spinach or Swiss chard, if using, and cook for 3 to 5 minutes, or till tender. Drain and keep warm.

Meanwhile, in a large saucepan or pasta pot bring 12 cups/3 qt/3 l water to boiling. Add pasta. Reduce heat slightly. Boil, uncovered, for 8 to 10 minutes for dried pasta or 1½ to 2 minutes for fresh pasta, or till al dente, stirring occasionally. (Or, cook according to package directions.) Drain immediately.

Meanwhile, in a large frying pan cook the pancetta in hot oil. (If using bacon, cook it without the oil.) Add onion to cooked pancetta or bacon and cook till tender. Stir in flour, sugar, salt, and pepper. Stir in chicken stock and vinegar all at once. Cook and stir till thickened and bubbly. Cook and stir for 2 minutes more. Stir in cooked greens and squash; mix well. Spoon mixture over hot cooked pasta. Serve immediately.

Per serving 255 calories/1,071 kilojoules, 8 g protein, 31 g carbohydrate, 11 g total fat (4 g saturated), 12 mg cholesterol, 535 mg sodium, 249 mg potassium

STEP 1

Preparing Greens
Cut along either side of the center rib of kale from top to bottom; discard the ribs and chop the leaves.

STEP 2

Dicing Pancetta
Make parallel cuts in one flat slice of pancetta. Turn the knife and slice across the cuts to form diced pieces.

STEP 3

Cooking Pancetta
Heat the oil, then add the diced pancetta. Cook until browned and crisp on the edges, tossing to keep the pieces from sticking.

Springtime Carbonara

We call this "springtime" because vegetables replace the bacon used in traditional carbonara. However, with fresh vegetables available all year round, you can enjoy this delicious carbonara during the winter, too.

INGREDIENTS

4 oz/125 g baby carrots

1 cup/5 oz/155 g frozen peas or shelled fresh peas

4 oz/125 g fresh asparagus, trimmed and cut into 2-in/5-cm pieces

6 oz/185 g dried spaghetti or fettuccine or 12 oz/375 g fresh fettuccine or other ribbon pasta

1 beaten egg

1 cup/8 fl oz/250 ml light (single) cream

2 tablespoons margarine or butter

1/2 cup/2 oz/60 g grated Parmesan cheese

2 tablespoons chopped fresh chives or scallions (spring onions)

pepper

Preparation Time 20 minutes
Cooking Time 18 to 19 minutes
Serves 6 as an accompaniment or first course

Strands of pasta twine around a colorful mixture of vegetables, all coated with a creamy sauce.

Ribbon Pasta

METHOD FOR MAKING SPRINGTIME CARBONARA

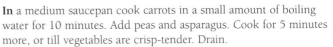

In a medium saucepan cook carrots in a small amount of boiling water for 10 minutes. Add peas and asparagus. Cook for 5 minutes more, or till vegetables are crisp-tender. Drain.

Meanwhile, in a large saucepan or pasta pot bring 12 cups/3 qt/3 l water to boiling. Add pasta. Reduce heat slightly. Boil, uncovered, 8 to 12 minutes for dried pasta or 1½ to 2 minutes for fresh, or till al dente, stirring occasionally. (Or, cook according to package directions.) Return pasta to warm pan; add cooked vegetables.

In a medium saucepan combine the egg, cream, and margarine or butter. Cook and stir over medium heat till mixture just coats a metal spoon (about 3 to 4 minutes). Do not boil, or the egg will curdle. Remove from heat. Immediately stir in the Parmesan cheese and chives or scallions. Pour egg mixture over hot pasta and vegetables and toss to coat pasta. Transfer to a warm serving dish. Sprinkle with pepper and serve immediately.

Per serving 276 calories/1,159 kilojoules, 11 g protein, 31 g carbohydrate, 12 g total fat (7 g saturated), 65 mg cholesterol, 229 mg sodium, 257 mg potassium

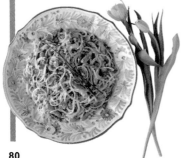

Ribbon Pasta

STEP 1

Testing Egg Mixture

Dip a spoon into the cooked egg mixture. The excess should drip off, leaving a creamy coating slightly thicker than milk. The coating should hold its shape when you wipe a finger across the back of the spoon.

STEP 2

Chopping Chives

Hold a bunch of chives with one hand (remove any damaged pieces). With kitchen scissors, snip off little tubes (about 1/4 in/6 mm long) into a small bowl.

Diavolo is synonymous with "spicy".
In this quick-to-assemble seafood dish,
mustard and chili oil provide the heat.

Pasta & Shrimp Diavolo

You can easily adjust the spiciness of this dish by increasing or decreasing
the amount of chili you use, or by adding crushed
red pepper flakes for a real kick.

INGREDIENTS

8 oz/250 g dried spaghetti,
linguine, or fettuccine or
1 lb/500 g fresh fettuccine
or linguine

4 oz/125 g broccoli florets

1 cup/8 fl oz/250 ml chicken stock

2 tablespoons cornstarch
(cornflour)

2 tablespoons Dijon-style mustard

2 tablespoons lemon juice

1 tablespoon drained capers

1 lb/500 g fresh shrimp (prawns),
peeled and deveined, or
12 oz/375 g frozen peeled and
deveined shrimp, thawed

2 tablespoons olive oil or
cooking oil

1/2 teaspoon hot chili oil or
1/8 teaspoon chili powder

lemon wedges (optional)

METHOD FOR MAKING PASTA & SHRIMP DIAVOLO

Preparation Time 25 minutes
Cooking Time 8 to 12 minutes
Serves 4 as a main course

STEPS AT A GLANCE	Page
Making pasta	12–31
Cutting ribbon pasta	65–69

In a large saucepan or pasta pot bring 12 cups/3 qt/3 l water to boiling. Add pasta. Reduce heat slightly. Boil, uncovered, 8 to 12 minutes for dried pasta or 1½ to 2 minutes for fresh, or till al dente, stirring occasionally. (Or, cook according to package directions.) Add the broccoli to the boiling dried pasta during the last 5 minutes of cooking time. Drain immediately. (If using fresh pasta, cook the broccoli separately in a small amount of boiling water for about 5 minutes, or until crisp-tender. Drain and add to cooked pasta.)

Meanwhile, in a small mixing bowl stir together chicken stock, cornstarch, mustard, lemon juice, and capers; set aside. In a large frying pan cook and stir shrimp in hot olive oil or cooking oil and chili oil or powder over medium-high heat for 1 minute. Stir stock mixture; carefully add to pan. Cook and stir till thickened and bubbly. Cook and stir for 2 minutes more, or till shrimp turn pink. Toss with pasta-broccoli mixture until heated through. If desired, garnish with lemon wedges.

Per serving 407 calories/1,709 kilojoules, 25 g protein, 51 g carbohydrate, 11 g total fat (2 g saturated), 131 mg cholesterol, 588 mg sodium, 408 mg potassium

STEP 1

Cutting Florets

Florets are the tightly closed heads that top each thick stalk of broccoli. Trim off the stalks and use them in another recipe. Halve or quarter the florets if large.

STEP 2

Peeling Shrimp

With kitchen scissors or a paring knife, cut the shell along the curve of the back from head to tail end. The shell and legs should peel off in one piece. To devein, pull out and discard the dark vein that runs along the back.

STEP 3

Cooking Shrimp

Add the stock mixture to the partially cooked shrimp in the frying pan. Cook and stir an additional 2 minutes, or until the shrimp turn pink and opaque.

Fettuccine with Gorgonzola-Tarragon Sauce

This pasta dish is rich with cream and the intense flavor of Gorgonzola. Offer some extra crumbled Gorgonzola with the pasta for the cheese-lovers at the table.

INGREDIENTS

4 oz/125 g dried or 8 oz/250 g fresh spinach fettuccine or linguine

1 tablespoon margarine or butter

1/2 cup/2 oz/60 g crumbled Gorgonzola cheese

1/4 cup/2 fl oz/60 ml light (single) cream

2 tablespoons chopped fresh tarragon or 1 1/2 teaspoons dried tarragon, crushed

dash ground white pepper or black pepper

1/4 cup/1 oz/30 g grated Parmesan cheese

2 tablespoons chopped toasted pecans or walnuts

Preparation Time 15 minutes
Cooking Time 8 to 10 minutes
Serves 4 as an accompaniment or first course

Tarragon and pungent blue-veined Gorgonzola add punch to this creamy sauce. A garnish of chopped toasted pecans provides a crunchy contrast.

METHOD FOR MAKING FETTUCCINE WITH GORGONZOLA-TARRAGON SAUCE

In a large saucepan or pasta pot bring 12 cups/3 qt/3 l water to boiling. Add pasta. Reduce heat slightly. Boil, uncovered, 8 to 10 minutes for dried pasta or 1½ to 2 minutes for fresh, or till al dente, stirring occasionally. (Or, cook according to package directions.) Drain immediately. Return pasta to warm pan.

Meanwhile, in a small saucepan melt margarine or butter. Add the Gorgonzola cheese, cream, tarragon, and pepper. Cook and stir over medium heat till cheese is melted and mixture is smooth and heated through. Stir in Parmesan cheese. Pour sauce over pasta. Gently toss till pasta is coated. Transfer to a warm serving dish. Sprinkle with nuts. Serve immediately with extra cheese if desired.

Per serving 253 calories/1,062 kilojoules, 10 g protein, 23 g carbohydrate, 13 g total fat (7 g saturated), 29 mg cholesterol, 377 mg sodium, 130 mg potassium

STEPS FOR CRUMBLING CHEESE AND TOASTING NUTS

STEP 1

Crumbling Gorgonzola

In order for the cheese to melt quickly and smoothly, it should be crumbled first. Put a chunk of cheese in a pie plate or on a dish. Crumble by breaking it up with a fork.

STEP 2

Toasting Nuts

Spread the nuts in a metal pie plate. Bake in a preheated 350°F/180°C/Gas Mark 4 oven for 5 to 10 minutes, or until lightly browned. Stir once or twice so the nuts brown evenly.

Fresh herb leaf pasta needs nothing more than a simple olive oil and garlic sauce to make an elegant and delicious first course.

Fresh Herb Leaf Pasta

This is different from pasta made with fresh chopped herbs. Here fresh herb leaves are pressed between two sheets of plain pasta. The result is delicate and delicious.

INGREDIENTS

1 lb/500 g homemade pasta (page 28)

1/2 oz/15 g each, dill, cilantro (fresh coriander), and flat-leaf parsley leaves, washed and carefully dried

1/3 cup/2 1/2 fl oz/75 ml olive oil

3 cloves garlic, finely chopped

2 tablespoons finely chopped flat-leaf parsley

freshly ground black pepper

Parmesan cheese shavings

Preparation time 20 minutes
Cooking time 3 minutes
Serves 6 as an accompaniment or first course

METHOD FOR MAKING FRESH HERB LEAF PASTA

Divide the pasta dough into 3 pieces. Cover 2 pieces with plastic wrap to prevent them from drying out. On a lightly floured surface, or using a pasta machine, roll out 1 piece into a very thin sheet. Distribute one-third of the herb leaves over half of the sheet. Carefully flatten each leaf in place. Lightly brush the uncovered half the sheet with water and fold it over the side with the leaves. Press down firmly to seal the leaves in and force out any air bubbles.

Roll the folded sheet through the pasta machine once to make a very thin sheet of pasta. With a sharp knife or pasta cutter, cut the sheet into 2-in/5-cm squares. Repeat the process with the remaining dough and leaves.

In a large saucepan or pasta pot bring 12 cups/3 qt/3 l water to boiling. Add pasta. Reduce heat slightly. Boil, uncovered, 1 1/2 to 2 minutes or until al dente.

Heat the oil in a frying pan. Add the garlic and cook gently for 1 minute. Add the parsley and pepper.

Drain the pasta. Toss through the oil and garlic. Garnish with Parmesan shavings. Serve immediately.

Per serving 362 calories/1,520 kilojoules, 10 g protein, 37 g carbohydrate, 19 g total fat (4 g saturated), 100 mg cholesterol, 151 mg sodium, 136 mg potassium

Aglio e Olio with Fresh Sage

Garlic (aglio) and oil (olio) are a classic Italian combination. When sage is added,
you have a light and delicious pasta sauce that can be made in a moment.

INGREDIENTS

4 oz/125 g mafalde, spaghetti, or
other dried ribbon pasta or
8 oz/250 g fresh fettuccine

2 tablespoons olive oil or
cooking oil

2 cloves garlic, minced

1 tablespoon chopped fresh
sage or 1/2 teaspoon
dried sage, crushed

salt and pepper

grated Parmesan cheese
(optional)

Preparation Time 10 minutes
Cooking Time 10 to 12 minutes
Serves 4 as an accompaniment or
first course

METHOD FOR MAKING AGLIO E OLIO WITH FRESH SAGE

Ruffled ribbon pasta in a garlicky sauce flecked with sage is the perfect accompaniment to roasted or grilled chicken.

In a large saucepan or pasta pot bring 12 cups/3 qt/3 l water to boiling. Add pasta. Reduce heat slightly. Boil, uncovered, for 10 to 12 minutes for dried pasta or 1½ to 2 minutes for fresh, or till al dente, stirring occasionally. (Or, cook according to package directions.) Drain immediately. Return pasta to warm pan.

Meanwhile, in a small saucepan heat oil over medium heat. Add garlic and sage and cook and stir for 1 minute.

Toss oil mixture with hot pasta. Season to taste with salt and pepper. If desired, sprinkle with Parmesan cheese. Serve immediately.

Per serving 175 calories/735 kilojoules, 4 g protein, 23 g carbohydrate, 7 g total fat (1 g saturated), 0 mg cholesterol, 35 mg sodium, 32 mg potassium

Straw & Hay with Wild Mushrooms in Cream

Pour a little of the boiling water from the pasta pot into your serving bowl to heat it up quickly. Empty the water just before you are ready to fill the bowl with pasta.

INGREDIENTS

4 oz/125 g dried or 8 oz/250 g fresh plain fettuccine

4 oz/125 g dried or 8 oz/250 g fresh spinach fettuccine

1 oz/30 g sliced scallions (spring onions)

4 oz/125 g finely chopped red or green pepper (capsicum)

3 tablespoons margarine or butter

6 oz/185 g fresh shiitake mushrooms, sliced

1 cup/8 fl oz/250 ml light (single) or heavy (double) cream

1/4 cup/1 oz/30 g grated Parmesan cheese

pepper

Preparation Time 15 minutes
Cooking Time 8 to 10 minutes
Serves 6 as an accompaniment or first course

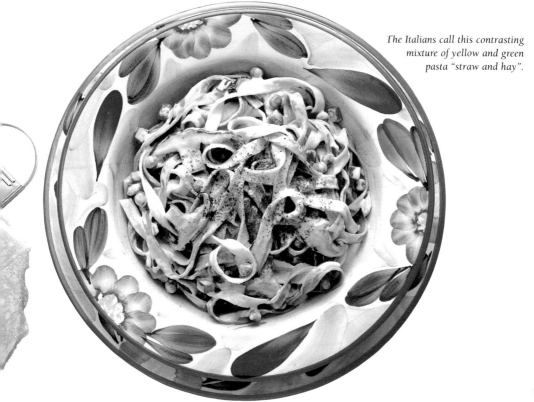

The Italians call this contrasting mixture of yellow and green pasta "straw and hay".

In a large saucepan or pasta pot bring 12 cups/3 qt/3 l water to boiling. Add pasta. Reduce heat slightly. Boil, uncovered, for 8 to 10 minutes for dried pasta or 1½ to 2 minutes for fresh, or till al dente, stirring occasionally. (Or, cook according to package directions.) Drain immediately. Return pasta to warm pan.

Meanwhile, in a large frying pan cook and stir scallions and red or green pepper in hot margarine or butter over medium-high heat for 2 minutes. Add mushrooms; cook and stir for 2 minutes more, or till vegetables are tender. Stir in cream and heat through, but do not let it boil.

Pour mushroom-cream mixture over pasta and toss to coat pasta. Add Parmesan cheese and toss. Transfer to a warm serving dish. Sprinkle with pepper. Serve immediately.

Per serving 277 calories/1,163 kilojoules, 9 g protein, 33 g carbohydrate, 12 g total fat (5 g saturated), 18 mg cholesterol, 170 mg sodium, 225 mg potassium

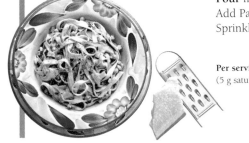

Fettuccine with Prosciutto & Radicchio

Bitter radicchio leaves are wilted by the heat of the pasta and fried prosciutto.
Fresh basil adds to the herby flavor.

INGREDIENTS

8 oz/250 g dried fettuccine or
1 lb/500 g fresh fettuccine

3¹/₂ oz/100 g butter

6¹/₂ oz/200 g prosciutto

2 tablespoons olive oil

¹/₃ oz/10 g finely shredded basil

8 leaves radicchio, washed and
finely shredded

1 cup/4 oz/125 g freshly grated
Parmesan cheese, plus extra
shavings, for garnish

freshly ground black pepper

Preparation Time 5 minutes
Cooking Time 15 minutes
Serves 6 as an accompaniment or
first course

STEPS AT A GLANCE	Page
▥ Making pasta	**12–31**
▥ Cutting ribbon pasta	**65–69**

This is very quick to make, especially if using fresh fettuccine. Rocket leaves can replace the radicchio if you find them too bitter.

METHOD FOR MAKING FETTUCCINE WITH
PROSCIUTTO & RADICCHIO

In a large saucepan or pasta pot bring 12 cups/3 qt/3 l water to boiling. Add pasta. Reduce heat slightly. Boil, uncovered, 8 to 12 minutes for dried pasta or 1½ to 2 minutes for fresh, or till al dente, stirring occasionally. (Or, cook according to package directions.) Drain well and return the pasta to the pan with the butter.

Fry the prosciutto in the olive oil till crisp. Drain on paper towels and then crumble.

In a bowl, combine the basil, radicchio, Parmesan, pepper and half the prosciutto.

Finally, add the pasta to the bowl and toss quickly and thoroughly through the sauce. Distribute among warmed pasta bowls, top with Parmesan shavings and the remaining prosciutto.

Per serving 579 calories/2,431 kilojoules, 21 g protein, 59 g carbohydrate, 29 g total fat (14 g saturated), 76 mg cholesterol, 1,031 mg sodium, 258 mg potassium

Sprinkle this seafood sauce with Parmesan cheese just before serving. It's always a good idea to grate a little extra to offer at the table.

Spaghetti with Creamy Clam Sauce

This creamy version of the ever-popular pasta with clam sauce cooks in minutes.
If small cans of minced clams are pantry staples, you can prepare an enticing meal
with very little notice. Serve with a green salad and crusty bread to soak up the sauce.

INGREDIENTS

8 oz/250 g dried spaghetti or
linguine or 1 lb/500 g fresh
linguine or other ribbon pasta

SAUCE

14 oz/440 g canned minced
clams or chopped cooked clams

light (single) cream or milk

2 oz/60 g chopped onion

2 cloves garlic, minced

2 tablespoons margarine
or butter

1/4 cup/1 oz/30 g all-purpose
(plain) flour

1/2 teaspoon dried basil or
oregano, crushed

1/4 teaspoon salt

1/4 teaspoon pepper

2 tablespoons chopped
fresh parsley

1/4 cup/2 fl oz/60 ml dry
white wine

1/4 cup/1 oz/30 g grated
Parmesan cheese

Preparation Time 20 minutes
Cooking Time 8 to 12 minutes
Serves 4 as a main course

In a large saucepan or pasta pot bring 12 cups/3 qt/3 l water to boiling. Add pasta. Reduce heat slightly. Boil, uncovered, for 8 to 12 minutes for dried pasta or 1½ to 2 minutes for fresh, or till al dente, stirring occasionally. (Or, cook according to package directions.) Drain.

Meanwhile, drain clams, reserving liquid. Add enough light cream or milk to the liquid to make 1¾ cups/14 fl oz/440 ml. (If using cooked clams, use 1¾ cups/14 fl oz/440 ml light cream or milk.)

For the sauce, in a medium saucepan cook the onion and garlic in hot margarine or butter for about 5 minutes, or till onion is tender but not brown. Stir in the flour, basil or oregano, salt, and pepper. Add the cream mixture all at once. Cook and stir till thickened and bubbly. Cook and stir for 1 minute more. Stir in the parsley, wine, and clams. Heat through.

Spoon sauce over hot pasta. Sprinkle with Parmesan cheese and serve immediately.

Per serving 551 calories/2,314 kilojoules, 21 g protein, 59 g carbohydrate, 25 g total fat (12 g saturated), 115 mg cholesterol, 401 mg sodium, 367 mg potassium

Turkey Tetrazzini

According to most accounts, the opera singer Luisa Tetrazzini inspired the original version of this poultry-based dish almost a century ago.

INGREDIENTS

6 oz/185 g dried spaghetti, vermicelli, or capellini or 12 oz/375 g fresh linguine

1 oz/30 g dried tomatoes (not oil-packed) (8 halves)

5 oz/155 g stemmed and sliced fresh shiitake mushrooms or button mushrooms

3 tablespoons margarine or butter

1/4 cup/1 oz/30 g all-purpose (plain) flour

1/8 teaspoon ground nutmeg

1 1/2 cups/12 fl oz/375 ml light (single) cream or milk

1 cup/8 fl oz/250 ml chicken stock

2 1/2 cups/15 oz/470 g chopped cooked turkey or chicken

2 tablespoons dry sherry

1/4 cup/1 oz/30 g grated Parmesan cheese

1/4 cup/1 oz/30 g flaked almonds

Preparation Time 25 minutes
Baking Time 20 minutes
Serves 6 as a main course

METHOD FOR MAKING TURKEY TETRAZZINI

In a large saucepan or pasta pot bring 12 cups/3 qt/3 l water to boiling. Add pasta. Reduce heat slightly. Boil, uncovered, 10 to 12 minutes for spaghetti, 5 to 7 minutes for vermicelli or capellini, or 1½ to 2 minutes for fresh pasta, or till al dente, stirring occasionally. (Or, cook according to package directions.) Drain immediately.

Place dried tomatoes in a small bowl. Add enough hot water to cover; soak for 10 to 15 minutes, or till softened. Drain and pat dry. Chop tomatoes; set aside.

Meanwhile, in a large saucepan cook mushrooms in melted margarine or butter till tender. Stir in flour and nutmeg. Add light cream or milk and chicken stock all at once. Cook and stir till thickened and bubbly. Stir in turkey or chicken, sherry, and chopped tomatoes. Add cooked pasta; toss to coat.

Transfer to an 8-cup/2-qt/2-l rectangular baking dish. Sprinkle with cheese and almonds. Bake in a preheated 350°F/180°C/Gas Mark 4 oven for 20 minutes, or till heated through. Serve immediately.

Per serving 462 calories/1,940 kilojoules, 29 g protein, 37 g carbohydrate, 22 g total fat (7 g saturated), 79 mg cholesterol, 481 mg sodium, 576 mg potassium

STEPS AT A GLANCE	Page
■ Cooking pasta	22–27

Use leftover cooked turkey or chicken for a pasta dish with all the flavors of an elegant pie.

Smoked turkey adds a subtle flavor to an elegant pasta sauce featuring both fresh and dried tomatoes.

Pasta with Turkey & Tomatoes in Cream

Grind fresh black pepper over the top of this savory pasta to give it a boost in flavor and in appearance. Garnish with Italian parsley.

INGREDIENTS

2 lb/1 kg ripe plum (Roma) tomatoes or 30 oz/940 g canned Italian-style tomatoes, cut up, with juice

2 cloves garlic, minced

1/2 teaspoon sugar

1/4 teaspoon salt

1/8 teaspoon pepper

1/2 cup/4 fl oz/125 ml heavy (double) cream

12 oz/375 g fully cooked smoked turkey breast, cut into 2x1/4 in/5-cmx6-mm strips

1/4 cup/2 oz/60 g drained oil-packed dried tomatoes, chopped

2 tablespoons chopped fresh parsley

8 oz/250 g fusilli, linguine, or other dried ribbon pasta or 1 lb/500 g fresh linguine or fettuccine

1/4 cup/1 oz/30 g grated Parmesan cheese (optional)

Preparation Time 20 minutes
Cooking Time 20 minutes
Serves 4 as a main course

METHOD FOR MAKING PASTA WITH TURKEY & TOMATOES IN CREAM

Peel and chop fresh plum tomatoes, if using. In a large frying pan heat oil over medium heat. Add fresh or undrained canned tomatoes, garlic, sugar, salt, and pepper. Bring to boiling; reduce heat. Boil gently, uncovered, for 15 minutes or till thickened, stirring occasionally. Gradually add the cream to the tomato mixture, stirring constantly. Add the turkey and dried tomatoes; heat through. Remove from heat; stir in parsley.

Meanwhile, in a large saucepan or pasta pot bring 12 cups/3 qt/3 l water to boiling. Add pasta. Reduce heat slightly. Boil, uncovered, 15 minutes for dried fusilli and 8 to 10 minutes for dried linguine, or 1½ to 2 minutes for fresh pasta, or till al dente, stirring occasionally. (Or, cook according to package directions.) Drain immediately.

Serve sauce over pasta. If desired, sprinkle with Parmesan cheese. Serve immediately.

Per serving 493 calories/2,070 kilojoules, 29 g protein, 63 g carbohydrate, 15 g total fat (8 g saturated), 77 mg cholesterol, 1,045 mg sodium, 1,076 mg potassium

Toasted Vermicelli with Fresh Salsa

To give the sauce even more of a Spanish flavor, use 1 cup/8 fl oz/250 ml of clam juice and 1 cup/8 fl oz/250 ml of chicken stock, instead of 2 cups/16 fl oz/500 ml of chicken stock. This makes a tasty complement for grilled fish.

INGREDIENTS

5 oz/155 g dried vermicelli or capellini, broken into 1/2-in/12-mm pieces

2 oz/60 g chopped onion

1 clove garlic, thinly sliced

2 tablespoons olive oil or cooking oil

2 tomatoes, peeled, seeded and chopped

2 cups/16 fl oz/500 ml chicken stock

3 small fresh chilies, seeded and thinly sliced

1/2 teaspoon dried oregano, crushed

1/4 teaspoon ground cumin

1/4 teaspoon salt

2 tablespoons chopped cilantro (fresh coriander)

chopped fresh tomatoes (optional)

METHOD FOR MAKING TOASTED VERMICELLI WITH FRESH SALSA

Preparation Time 25 minutes
Cooking Time 15 minutes
Serves 6 as an accompaniment
or first course

STEPS AT A GLANCE   Page

In a large frying pan cook pasta, onion, and garlic in hot oil for
5 minutes, or till pasta is golden and onion is tender, stirring
constantly. Gently stir in 2 tomatoes, the chicken stock, chilies,
oregano, cumin, and salt. Bring to boiling; reduce heat. Simmer,
uncovered, for about 8 minutes, or till pasta is al dente. Stir in
cilantro. Transfer to a serving dish. If desired, garnish with chopped
fresh tomatoes.

Per serving 166 calories/697 kilojoules, 6 g protein, 23 g carbohydrate, 6 g total fat
(1 g saturated), 0 mg cholesterol, 353 mg sodium, 239 mg potassium

In this unusual preparation, the vermicelli is first sautéed in oil, then cooked with the rest of the sauce.

Bucatini with Ginger Carrots

The inclusion of coconut milk, ginger and cilantro gives this dish an Asian flavor. Fresh or dried egg noodles can replace the bucatini if you prefer.

Bucatini, also known as "perciatelli", is a long, hollow pasta, like spaghetti, but thicker.

INGREDIENTS

1 lb/500 g carrots, cut into julienne

3 1/2 oz/100 g butter

2 teaspoons brown sugar

2 teaspoons white wine vinegar

1 tablespoon cumin seeds

1 teaspoon grated fresh ginger root

1/3 cup/2 1/2 fl oz/80 ml coconut milk

3 tablespoons finely chopped cilantro (fresh coriander)

8 oz/250 g bucatini or 1 lb/500 g fresh egg noodles or fettuccine

toasted sesame seeds, for garnish

Preparation time 10 minutes
Cooking time 20 minutes
Serves 4 as an accompaniment or first course

STEPS AT A GLANCE	Page
■ Making pasta	12–31
■ Cutting ribbon pasta	65–69

Steam carrots until just tender. Melt the butter in a frying pan and stir in the sugar and vinegar until the mixture is well combined. Add the cumin seeds and ginger and cook for a few minutes. Add the coconut milk and warm gently. Add the cooked carrots and cilantro and warm through.

Meanwhile, in a large saucepan or pasta pot bring 12 cups/3 qt/3 l water to boiling. Add pasta. Reduce heat slightly. Boil, uncovered, 8 to 12 minutes for bucatini, or 1 1/2 to 2 minutes for fresh pasta, or till al dente, stirring occasionally. (Or, cook according to package directions.) Drain and stir into the carrot mixture. Serve immediately in warmed bowls. Garnish with toasted sesame seeds.

Per serving 299 calories/1,255 kilojoules, 6 g protein, 36 g carbohydrate, 15 g total fat (12 g saturated), 43 mg cholesterol, 161 mg sodium, 308 mg potassium

Spaghetti & Meatballs

If you prefer not to brown the meatballs in a frying pan, you can bake them in a
preheated 375°F/190°C/Gas Mark 4 oven for about 20 minutes, or till no pink remains.
To make soft bread crumbs, shred the bread with a fork or process
briefly in a blender or food processor.

INGREDIENTS

classic tomato sauce (page 41)

1 beaten egg

3/4 cup/1 1/2 oz/45 g soft
bread crumbs

1 oz/30 g finely chopped onion

2 tablespoons finely chopped
green pepper (capsicum)

1/4 teaspoon salt

1/4 teaspoon dried oregano, crushed

1 lb/500 g lean ground (minced)
beef or pork sausage meat

1 tablespoon cooking oil

8 oz/250 g dried spaghetti or
linguine or 1 lb/500 g fresh linguine
or other ribbon pasta

Preparation Time 1 hour
(includes sauce)
Cooking Time 21 to 27 minutes
Serves 4 to 6 as a main course

Everyone's favorite pasta dish: tasty meatballs in a simple tomato sauce on a bed of spaghetti. Sprinkle with Parmesan if desired.

Prepare classic tomato sauce as directed; keep warm.

In a large mixing bowl combine egg, bread crumbs, onion, green pepper, salt, and oregano. Add beef or sausage meat; mix well. Shape into thirty 1-in/2.5-cm meatballs. In a large frying pan heat the oil and cook the meatballs, in 2 batches, for 8 to 10 minutes, or till no pink remains. Drain well. Add meatballs to the warm sauce. Cook, uncovered, for 5 minutes to heat through and blend flavors, stirring occasionally. Keep warm.

In a large saucepan or pasta pot bring 12 cups/3 qt/3 l water to boiling. Add pasta. Reduce heat slightly. Boil, uncovered, 8 to 12 minutes for dried pasta or 1½ to 2 minutes for fresh, or till al dente, stirring occasionally. (Or, cook according to package directions.) Drain immediately.

Serve sauce and meatballs over hot pasta.

Per serving 681 calories/2,860 kilojoules, 34 g protein, 73 g carbohydrate, 29 g total fat (8 g saturated), 123 mg cholesterol, 564 mg sodium, 1,372 mg potassium

Linguine with Spicy Chili Sauce & Beans

If you ordered this dish in the American Midwest, it would be called "five-way" chili because it contains pasta, chili, cheese, onions, and beans.

INGREDIENTS

8 oz/250 g dried linguine or spaghetti or 1 lb/500 g fresh linguine or other ribbon pasta

MEAT SAUCE

1 lb/500 g ripe plum (Roma) tomatoes or canned tomatoes, cut up, with juice

1 lb/500 g lean ground (minced) chicken, turkey, or beef

2 oz/60 g chopped onion

1 clove garlic, minced

8 oz/250 g canned or bottled Italian-style tomato sauce

1/4 cup/2 fl oz/60 ml chicken stock

1 tablespoon red wine vinegar

1 tablespoon chili powder

1/2 teaspoon ground allspice

1/4 teaspoon ground cinnamon

1/4 teaspoon salt

1/8 teaspoon ground red pepper (cayenne) (optional)

TOPPINGS

1 lb/500 g canned cannellini beans

1 oz/30 g thinly sliced scallions (spring onions)

1/2 cup/2 oz/60 g shredded Cheddar cheese or 1/4 cup/1 oz/30 g grated Parmesan cheese

Preparation Time 30 minutes
Cooking Time 20 to 25 minutes
Serves 4 to 6 as a main course

This surprising version of pasta and meat sauce features the bold flavors of chili.

In a large saucepan or pasta pot bring 12 cups/3 qt/3 l water to boiling. Add pasta. Reduce heat slightly. Boil, uncovered, for 8 to 12 minutes for dried pasta or 1½ to 2 minutes for fresh, or till al dente, stirring occasionally. Drain immediately.

Meanwhile, peel, seed, and chop fresh plum tomatoes, if using. In a large frying pan cook ground chicken, turkey or beef, onion, and garlic for 5 minutes, or till meat is brown and onion is tender. Drain off fat. Stir in fresh or undrained canned tomatoes, tomato sauce, chicken stock, vinegar, chili powder, allspice, cinnamon, salt, and, if desired, red pepper. Bring to boiling; reduce heat. Simmer, uncovered, for 15 to 20 minutes, or to desired consistency, stirring occasionally.

To serve, heat cannellini beans in a small saucepan; drain. Top hot cooked pasta with meat sauce, beans, scallions, and Cheddar or Parmesan cheese. Serve immediately.

Per serving 530 calories/2,226 kilojoules, 36 g protein, 74 g carbohydrate, 13 g total fat (5 g saturated), 69 mg cholesterol, 866 mg sodium, 993 mg potassium

Stir-fried Vegetables with Buckwheat Noodles

Pasta is wonderfully versatile: it's not just for meals with an Italian accent, as you'll see when you taste this Asian-style dish.

INGREDIENTS

4 oz/125 g dried buckwheat noodles (soba), Chinese egg noodles, or fine egg noodles

SAUCE

1/2 cup/4 fl oz/125 ml chicken stock

1 tablespoon cornstarch (cornflour)

1 tablespoon soy sauce

2 teaspoons sesame oil

VEGETABLES

1 tablespoon cooking oil

2 cloves garlic, cut into slivers (1 teaspoon)

2 teaspoons grated fresh ginger root

10 oz/315 g extra-firm tofu, drained and cut into thin strips

1 red or yellow pepper (capsicum), cut into thin strips

3 oz/90 g fresh snow peas (mangetout)

5 oz/155 g sliced yellow baby squash or zucchini (courgettes)

3 scallions (spring onions), bias-sliced into 1-in/2.5-cm pieces

Soba noodles, made from buckwheat, are a favorite in Japan and are enjoyed either hot or cold.

METHOD FOR MAKING
STIR-FRIED VEGETABLES WITH BUCKWHEAT NOODLES

Preparation Time 30 minutes
Cooking Time 16 to 17 minutes
Serves 4 as a main course

STEPS AT A GLANCE   Page
■ Cooking pasta   22–27

In a large saucepan or pasta pot bring 12 cups/3 qt/3 l water to boiling. Add buckwheat noodles or egg noodles. Reduce heat slightly. Boil, uncovered, 10 minutes for buckwheat noodles or 4 to 6 minutes for egg noodles, or till al dente, stirring occasionally. (Or, cook according to package directions.) Drain immediately.

Meanwhile, for sauce, in a small mixing bowl stir together chicken stock, cornstarch, soy sauce, and sesame oil; set aside.

For vegetables, in a large frying pan heat cooking oil over medium-high heat. Add garlic, ginger, and tofu. Cook for 2 minutes, or till tofu is heated through, turning tofu once. Remove from pan. Add red or yellow pepper, snow peas, yellow baby squash or zucchini, and scallions to skillet. Stir-fry for 2 to 3 minutes, or till crisp-tender. Push vegetables to sides of pan. Stir sauce and add to center of pan. Cook and stir till thickened and bubbly. Return tofu and noodles to pan. Stir all ingredients together to coat with sauce; heat through and serve immediately.

Per serving 231 calories/970 kilojoules, 13 g protein, 31 g carbohydrate, 8 g total fat (1 g saturated), 0 mg cholesterol, 602 mg sodium, 380 mg potassium

Szechwan Chicken & Pasta

Chinese egg noodles are made from wheat flour, water, and egg and are shaped either round or flat. They are available fresh or dried. Many well-stocked supermarkets carry fresh noodles in the refrigerator together with spring-roll wrappers. You can substitute any fresh ribbon pasta for the fresh Chinese noodles, if you prefer.

INGREDIENTS

1 lb/500 g boneless, skinless chicken breasts

6 oz/185 g fresh snow peas (mangetout)

1/4 cup/2 fl oz/60 ml soy sauce

2 tablespoons rice vinegar or white wine vinegar

1 teaspoon chili oil or sesame oil with 1/8 teaspoon chili powder

1/4 to 1/2 teaspoon crushed red pepper (chili) flakes

5 oz/155 g dried Chinese egg noodles or 8 oz/250 g fresh Chinese egg noodles

1 tablespoon cooking oil

2 cloves garlic, minced

1 large red or green pepper (capsicum), cut into thin strips

2 scallions (spring onions), sliced

1/4 cup/1 1/2 oz/45 g coarsely chopped peanuts

125

*This pasta meal is full of healthy
vegetables, low-fat chicken, and
a tangy mixture of soy sauce,
chili oil, and rice vinegar.*

METHOD FOR MAKING SZECHWAN CHICKEN & PASTA

Rinse chicken and pat dry. Cut into 3/4-in/2-cm pieces. Coarsely chop the snow peas. In a small bowl stir together the soy sauce, vinegar, chili oil, and crushed red pepper. Set aside.

For dried noodles, in a large saucepan or pasta pot bring 12 cups/ 3 qt/3 l water to boiling. Add noodles. Reduce heat slightly. Boil, uncovered, 4 to 6 minutes, or till tender, stirring occasionally. (Prepare fresh noodles according to package directions.) Drain.

Pour cooking oil into a wok or large frying pan. (Add more oil as necessary during cooking.) Preheat over medium-high heat. Stir-fry the garlic in hot oil for 15 seconds. Add the snow peas, red or green pepper, and scallions; stir-fry for 1 to 2 minutes, or till crisp-tender. Remove the vegetables from the wok.

Add half the chicken to the hot wok. Stir-fry for 2 to 3 minutes, or till no pink remains. Remove the chicken from the wok. Repeat with remaining chicken. Return all chicken to the wok. Add the soy sauce mixture to the wok. Add the cooked vegetables and noodles. Stir ingredients together to coat with soy sauce mixture. Cook and stir about 1 minute more, or till heated through. Sprinkle with peanuts. Serve immediately.

Preparation Time 25 minutes
Cooking Time 11 to 13 minutes
Serves 5 as a main course

STEPS AT A GLANCE	Page
▪ Cooking pasta	22–27

Per serving 369 calories/1,550 kilojoules, 27 g protein, 39 g carbohydrate, 12 g total fat (2 g saturated), 87 mg cholesterol, 910 mg sodium, 407 mg potassium

Summer Spaghetti

This dish combines hot spaghetti with a fresh salsa of tomatoes, onion, chili and olives. It makes a delicious and quick summer lunch.

INGREDIENTS

1 lb/500 g firm ripe tomatoes, peeled, seeded and finely chopped

1 red onion, diced

1 small red chili, seeded and finely chopped

12 stuffed green olives, finely chopped

1 tablespoon capers, chopped if large

1 1/2 teaspoons finely chopped fresh oregano

1/2 oz/15 g finely chopped parsley

2 cloves garlic, crushed

1/2 cup/4 fl oz/125 ml extra-virgin olive oil

8 oz/250 g dried spaghetti

Preparation Time 20 minutes
Cooking Time 12 minutes
Serves 4 as a main course

This unusual combination of hot spaghetti with a cold, spicy, fresh tomato salsa, needs no Parmesan.

METHOD FOR MAKING SUMMER SPAGHETTI

Combine tomatoes, red onion, chili, olives, capers, oregano, parsley, garlic, and oil in a bowl. Mix well; cover and let stand overnight.

In a large saucepan or pasta pot bring 12 cups/3 qt/3 l water to boiling. Add pasta. Reduce heat slightly. Boil, uncovered, 8 to 12 minutes, or till al dente, stirring ocasionally. (Or, cook according to package directions.) Drain. Serve sauce at room temperature over hot pasta.

Per serving 488 calories/2,049 kilojoules, 11 g protein, 62 g carbohydrate, 22 g total fat (3 g saturated), 0 mg cholesterol, 234 mg sodium, 337 mg potassium

Filipino-Style Noodles

Pancit canton noodles are a favorite in the Philippines, where pancit means "noodle". Because they are precooked and sold dried, they need only be added to boiling liquid for a brief time before they are tender.

INGREDIENTS

2 oz/60 g chopped onion

2 cloves garlic, minced

2 tablespoons cooking oil

4 oz/125 g thinly bias-sliced carrots

1 small zucchini (courgette), cut into short, thin strips

3 oz/90 g shredded cabbage

1 cup/8 fl oz/250 ml chicken stock

2 tablespoons soy sauce

5 oz/155 g cooked pork, sliced into thin strips

5 oz/155 g cooked shrimp (prawns), chopped

8 oz/250 g Pancit Canton noodles or dried
Chinese egg noodles

1 oz/30 g sliced scallions (spring onions)

Preparation Time 25 minutes
Cooking Time: 12 minutes
Serves 4 as a main course

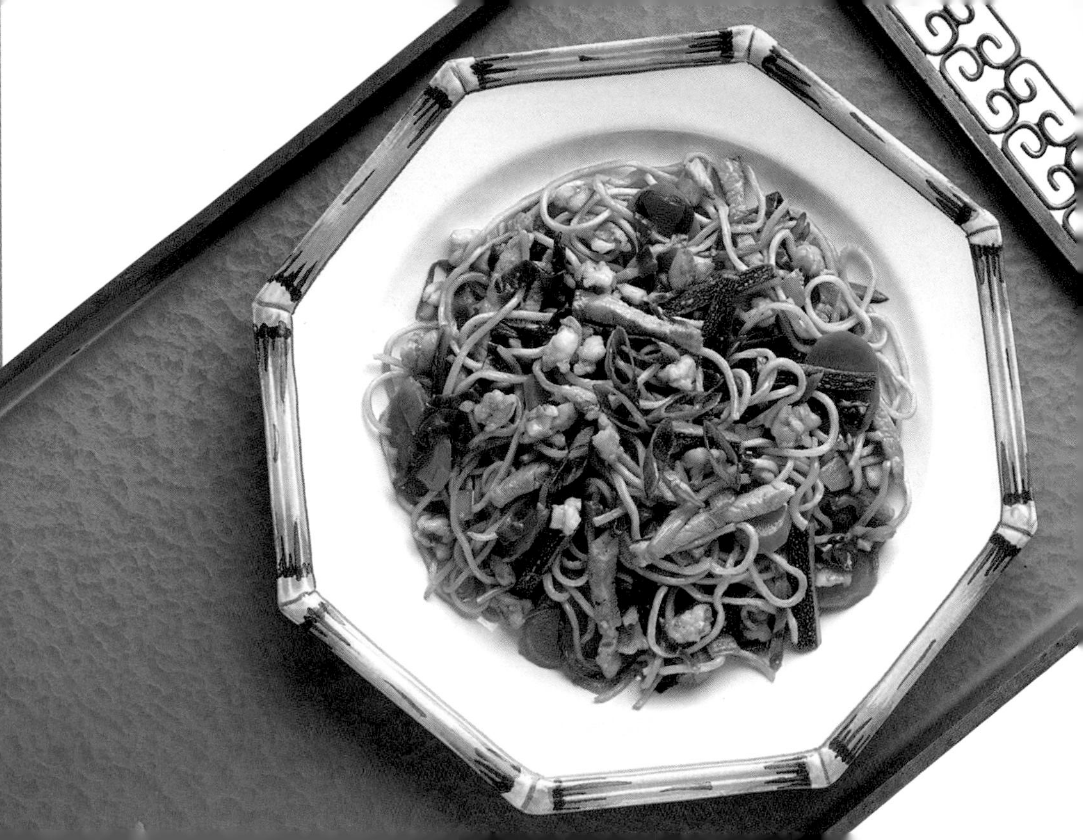

In a 12-in/30-cm frying pan cook onion and garlic in hot oil for 5 minutes, or till tender but not brown Add carrots, zucchini, cabbage, chicken stock, and soy sauce; mix well. Bring to boiling; reduce heat. Cover and simmer for 5 minutes, or till carrots are crisp-tender. Stir in pork and shrimp.

Break noodles apart and stir into cooked mixture. (If necessary, add additional chicken stock to cook noodles.) Cover and cook over low heat about 2 minutes for pancit canton noodles and 4 to 6 minutes for egg noodles, or till noodles are tender and liquid is absorbed. Stir mixture gently and transfer to a serving dish. If desired, sprinkle with scallions.

Per serving 407 calories/1,709 kilojoules, 22 g protein, 51 g carbohydrate, 12 g total fat (3 g saturated), 79 mg cholesterol, 1,861 mg sodium, 553 mg potassium

This stir-fry dish contains the same ingredients as egg roll stuffing, but here they are served with long wheat noodles.

SHAPED PASTA

BASIC TOOLS FOR MAKING SHAPED PASTA

Cut basic rectangles and circles for shaping from pasta dough with a fluted pastry wheel and a ruler, or a round biscuit cutter.

cutting board

biscuit cutter

fluted pastry wheel

ruler

Making Shaped Pasta

Only a very few of the hundreds of charming pasta shapes that are turned out so effortlessly in the factory can be formed by hand.

Farfalle, which to some resemble little butterflies and to others bow ties, may be the easiest to do. They begin as small rectangles of dough cut from a freshly rolled sheet. If you prefer them with a decoratively pinked edge, use a fluted pastry wheel to cut them. Otherwise, any sharp knife or a straight-edge pizza cutter will work well.

Tripolini are also described as bow ties, but rather than having crisp, straight edges and sharp, angular corners, they are rounded like the bow ties worn by circus clowns. They are formed in the same way as farfalle, but begin as circles rather than rectangles.

Orecchiette, "little ears", are thin cups said to have originated in Apulia, an Italian region that makes up the heel of Italy's boot. This is a wonderful pasta for sauces because it not only absorbs the sauce, but traps it inside the cup.

For any of these shapes, prepare homemade pasta dough, as directed (page 28), then follow the steps on pages 139 to 141.

MAKING SHAPED PASTA

Let the shaped pasta dry partially on a flour-dusted towel or baking sheet before cooking, or dry it completely if storing in the refrigerator. Turn occasionally to expose both sides to the air.

Homemade farfalle and tripolini will cook in 2 to 3 minutes. Orecchiette are thicker and take a little more time, 6 to 7 minutes. All three are available as packaged dried pastas, too. These pastas are delicious served hot with meat and vegetable sauces. Florentine-inspired Chicken Livers over Pasta, page 171, features chicken livers and farfalle or tripolini in a creamy sauce dotted with colorful pieces of red and green peppers. Orecchiette with Fennel in Parmesan Cream, page 177, is an anise-flavored combination of fresh fennel and Sambuca plus mushrooms and Italian prosciutto ham. These shapes are attractive additions to pasta salads as well. Warm Tomato–Feta Cheese Salad, page 301, is a refreshing summer dish that shows off farfalle – either fresh or dried.

you can also use a pizza wheel or a knife to cut the strips

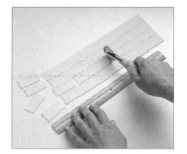

STEP 1

Making Farfalle (Bow Ties)

Roll the dough ⅟₁₆ in/2 mm thick and trim the sides so that they are straight and even. (A ruler helps to do this.) Using a fluted pastry wheel, cut the dough into 1-in/2.5-cm-wide strips. Then cut crosswise every 2 in/5 cm to form 2x1-in/5x2.5-cm rectangles.

if the pasta is too dry to hold the pinch, dab a little water in the center

STEP 2

Shaping Farfalle

To form the bow tie, pinch the center of the rectangle. To create a nice fold, first lay your index finger or little finger sideways in the center of the dough and pinch against it. Remove your finger and finish making the bow tie pinch.

STEPS FOR MAKING SHAPED PASTA

save and reroll
dough scraps to
make more pasta

STEP 3

Making Tripolini

Using a 1-in or 1¼-in/2.5-cm or 3-cm round cutter,
cut the dough into circles. Shape as for farfalle (step 2).
Pinch the center of each circle to form a rounded
bow tie.

don't flour the
work surface
or the dough too
heavily or the log
will slide instead
of rolling

STEP 4

Making Orecchiette

Shape 4 to 6 oz/125 to 185 g of pasta dough into a log
½ in/12 mm in diameter. Roll with even pressure to
avoid denting the dough and to keep it uniformly thick.

flour your hands as needed to keep the
pasta from sticking

STEP 5

Shaping Orecchiette

With a sharp knife, slice the roll
into ⅛-in/3-mm-thick slices. Place
one slice in your palm. Shape it into
a little cup by gently pressing the
middle of the slice with your index
finger. Twist your finger to broaden
the cup.

*Whimsical pasta shapes like farfalle
(bow ties), tripolini (rounded bow
ties), and orecchiette ("little ears")
are easily formed by hand.*

Dried Shaped Pasta

Nowhere is the playful side of the Italian character better illustrated than in the myriad shapes of dried pasta offered by commercial manufacturers. There are literally hundreds. Where else but in Italy would you eat food that looks like little radiators (radiatori) and cork-screws (fusilli), thimbles (ditali) and shells (conchiglie), bow ties (farfalle) and little ears (orecchiette), wheels (ruote) and rice or barley (orzo)! Often the same shape appears in several sizes (the smaller often ends in *ini* or *etti*, which are diminutives). For example, ditali are tubes about

½ in/12 mm long; ditalini are shorter. The same shape may be called one thing in one region and another elsewhere. One name can even be applied to more than one shape! Confusing, yes. A problem, not at all. Most shapes are interchangeable.

Dried shaped pasta complements sauces with large pieces of vegetables, similar in size to the pasta. Shells, spirals, and rigatoni go with meaty sauces because their indentations trap bits of ingredients. Small shells, elbow macaroni, and tubular ditali are good in soups.

to use with a sauce, cook shaped pasta in boiling water as shown on page 26

STEP 1

Adding Pasta to Boiling Stock

Bring a large pot of tasty stock to a rolling boil. Add pasta to the stock gradually, so that it keeps boiling. The pasta will absorb much of the cooking liquid, so be sure to use a generous amount of stock.

Dried pasta is available in a delightful array of shapes, including elbows, bow ties, wheels, tubes, and shells.

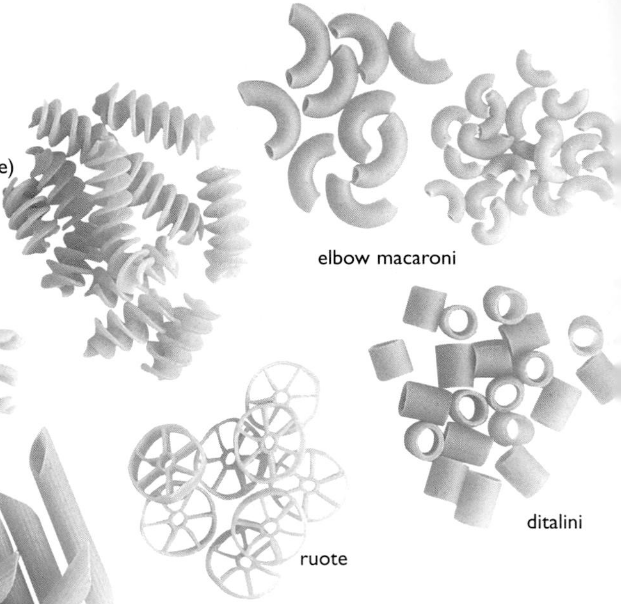

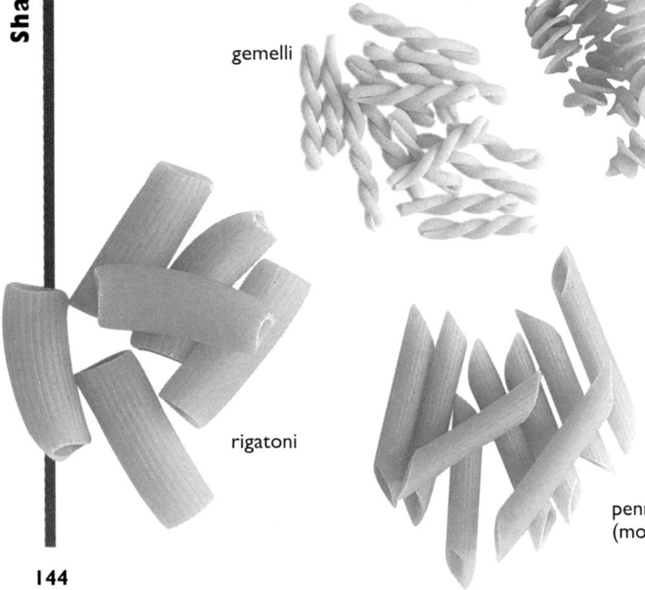

rotini
(rotelle)

gemelli

elbow macaroni

rigatoni

penne
(mostaccioli)

ruote

ditalini

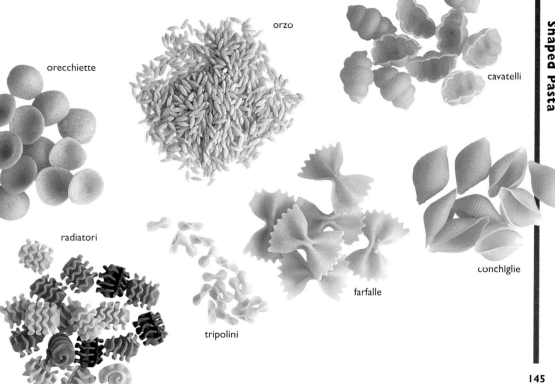

orzo

orecchiette

cavatelli

radiatori

farfalle

conchiglie

tripolini

When asparagus makes its long-awaited appearance in the spring, use the delicate vegetable to make this elegant main course.

Pasta & Shrimp in Asparagus Sauce

When setting aside asparagus pieces before puréeing, choose only the tips, which are usually the most tender part of the stalk and the most attractive.

INGREDIENTS

12 oz/375 g fresh or frozen shrimp (prawns), peeled and deveined

1 1/2 lb/750 g fresh asparagus spears

8 oz/250 g gemelli, rotini, or other dried shaped pasta

1 cup/8 fl oz/250 ml chicken stock

1/4 cup/2 fl oz/60 ml sour cream

2 tablespoons all-purpose (plain) flour

1/4 teaspoon salt

1/8 teaspoon white pepper

1 tablespoon lemon juice

Preparation Time 30 minutes
Cooking Time 15 minutes
Serves 4 as a main course

STEPS AT A GLANCE	Page
Cooking pasta	22–27
Peeling shrimp	85
Making asparagus sauce	149

Thaw shrimp, if frozen. Snap off and discard woody asparagus bases. Cut spears into 1½-in/4-cm pieces. Cook, covered, in a small amount of boiling water for 6 to 8 minutes, or till crisp-tender. Drain, reserving ¼ cup/2 fl oz/60 ml of the cooking liquid. Set aside 4 oz/125 g of the asparagus pieces; keep warm. In a blender container or food processor bowl, purée remaining asparagus with the reserved cooking liquid till nearly smooth, but still slightly chunky.

Meanwhile, in a large saucepan or pasta pot bring 12 cups/3 qt/3 l water to boiling. Add pasta. Reduce heat slightly. Boil, uncovered, for 8 to 10 minutes. Add shrimp to boiling pasta during the last 3 minutes of cooking. Cook till pasta is al dente and shrimp turn pink, stirring occasionally. (Or, cook according to package directions, adding shrimp for the last 3 minutes.) Drain immediately. Return pasta and shrimp to warm pan; add asparagus pieces.

In a medium saucepan stir together chicken stock, sour cream, flour, salt, and pepper. Add asparagus purée and lemon juice. Cook and stir over medium heat till thickened and bubbly. Cook and stir for 1 minute more. Pour sauce over hot pasta mixture and toss to coat. Serve immediately. This dish doesn't require Parmesan cheese.

Per serving 356 calories/1,495 kilojoules, 24 g protein, 53 g carbohydrate, 5 g total fat (2 g saturated), 116 mg cholesterol, 465 mg sodium, 497 mg potassium

STEP 1

Preparing Asparagus

Hold the asparagus stalk in both hands and press with your thumbs toward the thicker end. Snap off the woody base and discard.

STEP 2

Making Purée

Cook asparagus pieces in boiling water until crisp-tender. Blend all but 4 oz/125 g with the reserved cooking water in a blender or food processor to a chunky purée.

Artichokes, Lamb & Orzo Avgolemono

Avgolemono, a Greek sauce made with lemon juice and egg, is the base for this
Mediterranean-style lamb and artichoke topping for orzo pasta.
Try leg of lamb, fillet, or shoulder for lean cuts of lamb.

INGREDIENTS

2 tablespoons olive oil or cooking oil

1 lb/500 g boneless lean lamb, cut into
3/4-in/2-cm cubes

4 oz/125 g chopped onion

1 garlic clove, minced

3/4 cup/6 fl oz/185 ml white wine or
chicken stock

1 1/2 teaspoons chopped fresh oregano or
1/2 teaspoon dried oregano, crushed

1 teaspoon finely shredded lemon peel

1/4 teaspoon salt

1/4 teaspoon pepper

6 fresh medium artichokes, trimmed,
halved, and blanched, or 9 oz/280 g
frozen artichoke hearts

8 oz/250 g orzo

1 beaten egg

2 tablespoons lemon juice

1 tablespoon cornstarch (cornflour)

1/2 cup/4 fl oz/125 ml warm chicken stock

2 tablespoons chopped fresh parsley
(optional)

Artichokes and lamb combine in a Greek-inspired sauce served over tiny pasta that resembles grains of barley.

METHOD FOR MAKING ARTICHOKES, LAMB & ORZO AVGOLEMONO

Preparation Time 20 minutes
Cooking Time 45 minutes
Serves 4 as a main course

In a cooking pot or large frying pan heat the oil and brown half the lamb; remove meat. Brown remaining meat with onion and garlic till onion is tender. Drain fat from all the meat. Return all the meat to pan. Stir in ¾ cup/6 fl oz/185 ml wine or chicken stock, oregano, lemon peel, salt, and pepper. Bring to boiling; reduce heat. Cover; simmer for 20 minutes. Add artichokes and simmer 10 minutes more, or till tender (frozen artichoke hearts will cook in less time).

Meanwhile, in a large saucepan or pasta pot bring 12 cups/3 qt/3 l water to boiling. Add pasta. Reduce heat slightly. Boil, uncovered, for 5 to 8 minutes, or till al dente, stirring occasionally. (Or, cook according to package directions.) Drain immediately. Return to warm pan and keep warm.

Combine egg, lemon juice, cornstarch, and ½ cup/4 fl oz/125 ml warm chicken stock in a small mixing bowl. Pour egg mixture into lamb mixture. Cook and stir over medium heat for 1 minute, or till thickened and bubbly. Cook and stir for 2 minutes more. Serve lamb mixture over hot cooked pasta. If desired, garnish with parsley.

Per serving 525 calories/2,205 kilojoules, 31 g protein, 61 g carbohydrate, 15 g total fat (3 g saturated), 111 mg cholesterol, 356 mg sodium, 661 mg potassium

STEP 1

Trimming Artichokes
Trim stem flush with bottom. Break off tough outer leaves until only soft ones with a tinge of yellow remain.

STEP 2

Removing Chokes
Trim leaves to about 1 in/2.5 cm long. Cut artichoke in half to expose the choke. Scoop out the hairy choke with a tiny spoon or a melon baller and discard.

STEP 3

Adding Hearts to Water
Fill a bowl with water and squeeze lemon juice into it, then drop in some lemon slices to prevent artichokes from browning. Float trimmed artichoke hearts in acidulated water until needed.

Stuff colorful peppers with a Middle Eastern filling of spice-scented ground lamb and orzo instead of the usual rice.

Stuffed Peppers with Orzo

Orzo is a barley-shaped pasta frequently used in recipes as a substitute for rice.
Here it cooks in the stuffing mixture, saving the step of cooking the pasta separately.

INGREDIENTS

2 large red, yellow, and/or green peppers (capsicums)

12 oz/375 g ground (minced) lamb, turkey, or pork

1 oz/30 g chopped onion

8 oz/250 g canned Italian-style tomatoes, chopped

2 oz/60 g orzo

1 tablespoon chopped fresh mint, basil, or oregano, or
1/2 teaspoon dried mint, basil, or oregano, crushed

1/2 teaspoon ground allspice

1/2 cup/4 fl oz/125 ml water

1/4 teaspoon salt

1/4 teaspoon pepper

1/2 cup/2oz/60 g grated Parmesan cheese

Preparation Time 20 minutes
Baking Time 15 minutes
Serves 4 as a main course

Halve peppers lengthwise, removing stem ends, seeds, and membranes. Immerse peppers in boiling water for 3 minutes. Remove and sprinkle insides with salt. Invert peppers on paper towels to drain well.

In a frying pan cook lamb, turkey, or pork and onion for 5 minutes, or till meat is brown and onion is tender. Drain fat. Stir in tomatoes, uncooked pasta, mint, basil, or oregano, allspice, water, salt, and pepper. Bring to boiling; reduce heat. Cover and simmer for 7 to 8 minutes, or till pasta is al dente. Stir in half the Parmesan cheese. Fill peppers with meat mixture.

Place in a 8-cup/2-qt/2-l square baking dish with any remaining meat mixture. Bake in a preheated 375°F/190°C/Gas Mark 4 oven for about 15 minutes, or till heated through. Sprinkle with remaining cheese. Let stand for 1 to 2 minutes before serving.

Per serving 327 calories/1,373 kilojoules, 24 g protein, 22 g carbohydrate, 16 g total fat (8 g saturated), 68 mg cholesterol, 458 mg sodium, 509 mg potassium

STEP 1

Draining Peppers

Drop stemmed and seeded pepper halves in boiling water for several minutes to soften. Remove from the water with tongs, sprinkle the insides with salt, and drain, cut-side down, on paper towels.

STEP 2

Stuffing Peppers

Prepare the meat mixture, add the orzo, and cook till tender. Add cheese. Turn the peppers cut-side up. Spoon one quarter of the filling into each pepper half. Transfer to a baking dish.

Pasta with Tapenade

Tapenade, a purée of olives, capers, and anchovies, is generally offered as an appetizer
served with bread, but it also makes a splendid main course when tossed with hot pasta.

INGREDIENTS

8 oz/250 g cavatelli, conchiglie, or other dried shaped pasta

1/2 a fennel bulb or 2 oz/60 g celery, bias-sliced 1/4 in/6 mm thick

1/2 a red pepper (capsicum), cut into thin bite-size strips

1/2 a yellow pepper (capsicum), cut into thin bite-size strips

4 oz/125 g pitted black Greek olives, Niçoise olives, or pitted ripe olives

3 1/2 oz/105 g tuna, canned in water, drained

1 tablespoon capers, drained

1/2 teaspoon dried oregano or thyme, crushed

1 teaspoon anchovy paste (optional)

1 clove garlic

1 tablespoon olive oil or cooking oil

1 to 2 teaspoons lemon juice

2 tablespoons chopped fresh parsley

The sunny flavors and colors of the Mediterranean are captured in this sauce.

METHOD FOR MAKING PASTA WITH TAPENADE

Preparation Time 20 minutes
Cooking Time 12 to 14 minutes
Serves 4 as a main course

In a large saucepan or pasta pot bring 12 cups/3 qt/3 l water to boiling. Add pasta. Reduce heat slightly. Boil, uncovered, for 12 to 14 minutes, or till pasta is al dente, stirring occasionally. Add fennel and red and yellow peppers during the last 2 minutes of cooking. (Or, cook according to package directions, adding fennel and peppers for the last 2 minutes.) Drain immediately. Return pasta-vegetable mixture to warm pan.

Meanwhile, in a food processor bowl or blender container place the olives, tuna, capers, oregano or thyme, anchovy paste (if desired), garlic, and oil. Process or blend till mixture is smooth. Add lemon juice to taste. Add tuna mixture and parsley to hot cooked pasta mixture and toss to coat. Serve immediately.

Per serving 315 calories/1,323 kilojoules, 15 g protein, 49 g carbohydrate, 8 g total fat (1 g saturated), 4 mg cholesterol, 138 mg sodium, 187 mg potassium

STEP 1

Cutting Fennel

Trim away the feathery stalks just above where the bulb begins.
Leave the root end on. If necessary, remove any damaged outer stalks.

STEP 2

Slicing Fennel

Cut the trimmed bulb in half. Rinse between the layers to remove any grit.
Lay one half on a cutting board, cut-side down. Cut into 1/4-in/6-mm-thick
slices with a sharp knife.

Tomatoes, garlic and red peppers are roasted and then puréed to make a thick, rich sauce.

Rigatoni with Roasted Tomato, Red Pepper & Garlic

A dish incorporating all the tastes of southern Italy: tomatoes, red peppers, garlic, olive oil and olives.

INGREDIENTS

4 ripe tomatoes

1 large red pepper (capsicum), quartered, seeds and membrane removed

1 small head (bulb) garlic, excess paper skin removed

1 tablespoon olive oil

1 tablespoon balsamic vinegar

freshly ground black pepper

8 oz/250 g rigatoni, penne, or other dried shaped pasta

3 1/2 oz/100 g sun-dried tomatoes, chopped

3 1/2 oz/100 g/ Niçoise olives or other small black olives

Preparation Time 10 minutes
Cooking Time 45 minutes
Serves 4 as a main course

STEPS AT A GLANCE	Page
■ Cooking pasta	22–27

METHOD FOR MAKING RIGATONI WITH
ROASTED TOMATO, RED PEPPER & GARLIC

Preheat oven to 350°F/180°C/Gas Mark 4. Place the tomatoes, red pepper and garlic in a baking pan, brush with the oil and bake for 30 mintues.

Remove from the oven and set aside to cool slightly. Squeeze the garlic out of its skin, peel the tomatoes and red pepper and place all in a food processor with the vinegar. Process until the mixture is almost smooth but still has some texture. Add pepper.

Meanwhile in a large saucepan or pasta pot, bring 12 cups/3 qt/3 l water to boiling. Add pasta. Reduce heat slightly. Boil, uncovered, for 12 to 15 minutes, or till al dente, stirring occasionally. (Or, cook according to package directions.) Drain immediately.

Heat the sauce in a saucepan. Add the sun-dried tomatoes and black olives and warm through. Stir into the pasta and serve immediately in warmed pasta bowls.

Per serving 383 calories/1,608 kilojoules, 13 g protein, 77 g carbohydrate, 7 g total fat (0.9 g saturated), 0 g cholesterol, 121 mg sodium, 716 mg potassium

Scallops & Penne in Red Sauce

Watch the scallops carefully as they cook, and remove them the second they become opaque, or they will quickly become rubbery.

INGREDIENTS

12 oz/375 g fresh or frozen scallops

8 oz/250 g penne, rigatoni, or other dried shaped pasta

2 cloves garlic, minced

2 tablespoons olive oil or cooking oil

1/2 cup/4 fl oz/125 ml vermouth or red wine

2 teaspoons cornstarch (cornflour)

2 lb/1 kg ripe plum (Roma) tomatoes, peeled, seeded, and finely chopped

4 oz/125 g bottled diced pimiento, drained

2 tablespoons chopped fresh parsley

2 tablespoons chopped fresh basil

1/2 teaspoon salt

1/4 teaspoon crushed red pepper (chili) flakes

1/4 cup/1 oz/30 g grated Parmesan cheese (optional)

METHOD FOR MAKING SCALLOPS & PENNE IN RED SAUCE

Preparation Time 30 minutes
Cooking Time 20 minutes
Serves 4 as a main course

STEPS AT A GLANCE   Page

Thaw scallops, if frozen. In a large saucepan or pasta pot bring 12 cups/3 qt/3 l water to boiling. Add pasta. Reduce heat slightly. Boil, uncovered, for 14 to 15 minutes, or till al dente, stirring occasionally. (Or, cook according to package directions.) Drain.

Meanwhile, halve the scallops, if large. In a large frying pan cook and stir the garlic in hot oil for 1 minute. Add the scallops. Cook and stir for 2 minutes more, or till scallops are opaque. Remove scallops from pan; keep warm.

In the frying pan stir together the vermouth or red wine and cornstarch. Stir in tomatoes, pimiento, parsley, basil, salt, and red pepper. Cook and stir till thickened and bubbly. Reduce heat and cook and stir for 2 minutes more. Add hot cooked pasta and scallops and toss to coat with tomato mixture. Serve immediately with Parmesan cheese, if desired.

Per serving 409 calories/1,718 kilojoules, 20 g protein, 55 g carbohydrate, 9 g total fat (1 g saturated), 25 mg cholesterol, 417 mg sodium, 651 mg potassium

Long, narrow tubes of penne provide an attractive visual contrast to rounds of succulent scallops and pieces of chopped tomato.

Shaped Pasta

Pesto Pasta with Vegetables

Bring the pesto to room temperature if you've had it stored in the refrigerator
or freezer. Or, substitute purchased pesto for homemade.

INGREDIENTS

1/4 cup/2 fl oz/60 ml pesto
(page 49)

8 oz/250 g whole tiny new
potatoes

6 oz/185 g green beans

4 oz/125 g radiatori, rotini, or
other dried shaped pasta

1 to 2 tablespoons water

2 tablespoons grated Parmesan
cheese

Preparation Time 35 minutes
(includes pesto)
Cooking Time 8 to 12 minutes
Serves 4 as an accompaniment or
first course

STEPS AT A GLANCE	Page
▓ Cooking pasta	22–27
▪ Making pesto	49

When you bite into crinkly radiatori, they release a burst of the sauce trapped in their deep folds.

Prepare pesto as directed. Set aside.

Cut potatoes into halves if very small or into bite-size pieces. Cut green beans into 2-in/5-cm pieces. In a medium saucepan cook potatoes and green beans in a small amount of boiling salted water for about 10 minutes, or till vegetables are tender. Drain well.

Meanwhile, in a large saucepan or pasta pot bring 12 cups/3 qt/3 l water to boiling. Add pasta. Reduce heat slightly. Boil, uncovered, for 8 to 12 minutes, or till al dente, stirring occasionally. (Or, cook according to package directions.) Drain immediately. Return pasta to warm pan. Add potatoes and green beans.

In a small mixing bowl stir together pesto and enough of the water to make a thick sauce consistency. Pour the pesto mixture and Parmesan cheese over the pasta and vegetables and toss to coat. Serve immediately.

Per serving 274 calories/1,150 kilojoules, 10 g protein, 40 g carbohy-drate, 9 g total fat (2 g saturated), 7 mg cholesterol, 154 mg sodium, 471 mg potassium

Chicken Livers over Pasta

Italian cooks, particularly Florentines, adore chicken livers. One of the many good culinary uses to which they put them is this rich and hearty sauce for pasta. They're served with shaped pasta so that you can pick up a delicious morsel of liver with each bite.

INGREDIENTS

8 oz/250 g dried or 1 lb/500 g fresh farfalle or tripolini

12 oz/375 g chicken livers, cut in half

2 tablespoons margarine or butter

1 oz/30 g sliced scallion (spring onion)

1 1/2 oz/45 g chopped green pepper (capsicum)

1 1/2 oz/45 g chopped red pepper (capsicum)

1/2 cup/2 oz/60 g all-purpose (plain) flour

1/4 teaspoon salt

1/4 teaspoon pepper

1 1/3 cups/10 fl oz/315 ml chicken stock

2/3 cup/5 fl oz/160 ml light (single) cream or milk

1 tablespoon chopped fresh sage

Dress up chicken livers by serving them with pasta shaped like little bow ties.

METHOD FOR MAKING CHICKEN LIVERS OVER PASTA

Preparation Time 25 minutes
Cooking Time 10 minutes
Serves 4 as a main course

STEPS AT A GLANCE	Page
▨ Making pasta	12–31
■ Making shaped pasta	136–141

In a large saucepan or pasta pot bring 12 cups/3 qt/3 l water to boiling. Add pasta. Reduce heat slightly. Boil, uncovered, 10 minutes for dried farfalle (5 to 6 minutes for dried tripolini) or 2 to 3 minutes for fresh, or till al dente, stirring occasionally. (Or, cook according to package directions.) Drain immediately. Return pasta to warm pan.

Meanwhile, in a large frying pan cook chicken livers in hot margarine or butter over medium-high heat, turning as needed, for 4 to 5 minutes, or till centers are just slightly pink. Remove from pan; keep warm. Reserve pan drippings.

In the same pan cook the scallion and green and red peppers in the pan drippings for 2 to 3 minutes, or till tender. Stir in flour, salt, and pepper. Add chicken stock, light cream or milk, and sage. Cook and stir till thickened and bubbly. Cook and stir for 1 minute more. Pour sauce over hot cooked pasta and toss to coat. Add chicken livers; toss gently. Serve immediately.

Per serving 475 calories/1,995 kilojoules, 24 g protein, 53 g carbohydrate, 18 g total fat (7 g saturated), 359 mg cholesterol, 503 mg sodium, 290 mg potassium

Piselli e Pasta (Peas & Pasta)

Mascarpone is a buttery, rich and delicately flavored soft cheese from Italy.
A suitable substitute is ½ cup/4 oz/125 g of cream cheese blended
with 1 tablespoon of margarine or butter.

INGREDIENTS

4 oz/125 g conchiglie, cavatelli, or other dried shaped pasta

1 oz/30 g pancetta or bacon, finely chopped

1½ oz/45 g thinly sliced scallions (spring onions)

2 tablespoons margarine or butter

1 cup/5 oz/155 g frozen small peas

1 tablespoon water

½ cup/4 oz/125 g mascarpone cheese

salt and pepper (optional)

1 to 2 tablespoons milk (optional)

STEPS AT A GLANCE	Page
▓ Cooking pasta	22–27

Preparation Time 20 minutes
Cooking Time 12 to 14 minutes
Serves 6 as an accompaniment or first course

Inspired by a Venetian classic made with peas and rice, this seasoned pasta side dish is an ideal accompaniment to roasted fowl.

In a large saucepan or pasta pot bring 12 cups/3 qt/3 l water to boiling. Add pasta. Reduce heat slightly. Boil, uncovered, for 12 to 14 minutes, or till al dente, stirring occasionally. (Or, cook according to package directions.) Drain immediately.

Meanwhile, in a medium saucepan cook and stir pancetta, if using, and onions in hot margarine or butter for 2 minutes, or till onion is tender, but not brown. (If using bacon, omit margarine or butter and cook with onions as directed.) Add frozen peas and water to saucepan. Cover and simmer for 3 minutes. Gently stir in mascarpone cheese till melted. If desired, season to taste with salt and pepper. Add hot cooked pasta and toss to coat with cheese mixture. If mixture is too thick, add milk to thin to desired consistency. Serve immediately.

Per serving 178 calories/747 kilojoules, 6 g protein, 19 g carbohydrate, 9 g total fat (5 g saturated), 24 mg cholesterol, 88 mg sodium, 76 mg potassium

Orecchiette with Fennel in Parmesan Cream

Translated from the Italian, orecchiette means "little ears," a good description of their appearance. This is a very appealing pasta that can be made by hand (see pages 140 and 141) or purchased dried. Here it combines with a complex sauce that features exotic mushrooms and strips of Italian ham.

INGREDIENTS

4 oz/125 g dried or 8 oz/250 g fresh orecchiette

1 fennel bulb

3 to 4 oz/90 to 125 g fresh shiitake mushrooms

3 tablespoons margarine or butter

2½ oz/75 g finely chopped onion

2 oz/60 g prosciutto, cut into thin bite-size strips

¾ oz/20 g chopped fresh parsley

½ cup/4 fl oz/125 ml heavy (double) cream

½ cup/2oz/60 g grated Parmesan cheese

¼ cup/2 fl oz/60 ml chicken stock

1 beaten egg

1 tablespoon Sambuca or other anise liqueur or ½ teaspoon anise essence

½ teaspoon aniseed

*Anise liqueur and aniseed add
an unexpected note of licorice to
a sophisticated combination of
vegetables and prosciutto.*

Preparation Time 20 minutes
Cooking Time 10 minutes
Serves 6 as an accompaniment or
first course

In a large saucepan or pasta pot bring 12 cups/3 qt/3 l water to boiling. Add pasta. Reduce heat slightly. Boil, uncovered, 9 to 12 minutes for dried pasta or 2 to 3 minutes for fresh, or till al dente, stirring occasionally. (Or, cook according to package directions.) Drain.

Meanwhile, clean, trim, and slice the fennel bulb. Clean mushrooms; remove stems and discard. Slice mushroom caps.

In a large frying pan cook and stir the fennel over medium-high heat in hot margarine or butter for 3 minutes. Add the mushrooms and onion. Cook and stir for 5 minutes more. Add prosciutto and chopped parsley.

In a small mixing bowl combine cream, Parmesan cheese, chicken stock, egg, anise liqueur or anise essence, and aniseed. Pour cream mixture into frying pan. Cook and stir till cheese melts and sauce thickens slightly. Add hot cooked pasta and toss to coat pasta well. Serve immediately.

Per serving 298 calories/1,252 kilojoules, 11 g protein, 20 g carbohydrate, 19 g total fat (8 g saturated), 69 mg cholesterol, 450 mg sodium, 212 mg potassium

Broccoli, Sausage & Shells in Balsamic Sauce

Italian balsamic vinegar is aged for years in wooden barrels to mellow and sweeten. Look for this unique condiment in gourmet food shops and well-stocked supermarkets.

INGREDIENTS

6 oz/185 g conchiglie, cavatelli, or other dried shell-shaped pasta

8 oz/250 g broccoli florets

12 oz/375 g hot Italian-style sausages

1 tablespoon olive oil or cooking oil

2 cloves garlic, peeled

1 tablespoon all-purpose (plain) flour

1/8 to 1/4 teaspoon crushed red pepper (chili) flakes

1 cup/8fl oz/250 ml chicken stock

2 tablespoons balsamic vinegar

Preparation Time 20 minutes
Cooking Time 22 to 23 minutes
Serves 4 as a main course

STEPS AT A GLANCE	Page
▦ Cooking pasta	22–27
▦ Cutting florets	85

Lovers of spicy food will relish the fiery jolt provided by hot Italian sausage and crushed dried chili.

METHOD FOR MAKING
BROCCOLI, SAUSAGE & SHELLS IN BALSAMIC SAUCE

In a large saucepan or pasta pot bring 12 cups/3 qt/3 l water to boiling. Add pasta. Reduce heat slightly. Boil, uncovered, for 12 to 14 minutes, or till pasta is al dente, stirring occasionally. Add broccoli to the pan during the last 5 minutes of cooking. (Or, cook according to package directions, adding broccoli for the last 5 minutes.) Drain. Return pasta and broccoli to warm pan.

Meanwhile, in a large frying pan cook sausages, covered, in ½ cup/4 fl oz/125 ml boiling water for 15 minutes. Drain off liquid. Add olive oil and garlic to sausages in pan and cook, uncovered, for 4 to 5 minutes, turning sausages to brown them on all sides. Remove from heat. Discard garlic and reserve 1 tablespoon of the pan drippings in the pan. Cool sausages, then bias-slice into ¼-in/6-mm-thick pieces.

Stir flour and crushed red pepper into reserved drippings in pan. Add chicken stock all at once. Cook and stir over medium heat till thickened and bubbly. Cook and stir for 2 minutes more. Stir in balsamic vinegar. Pour chicken stock mixture over pasta-broccoli mixture. Add sausages and toss to mix well and heat through. Serve immediately.

Per serving 460 calories/1,932 kilojoules, 23 g protein, 45 g carbohydrate, 21 g total fat (6 g saturated), 49 mg cholesterol, 804 mg sodium, 629 mg potassium

Rigatoni with
Sausage & Mushroom Sauce

**Rib-sticking and chunky, this is an ideal cold-weather meal, perfect
for serving after winter sports. Serve with a glass of red wine.**

INGREDIENTS

1 lb/500 g Italian-style sausage
meat (casings removed)

3 oz/90 g sliced fresh
mushrooms

2 oz/60 g chopped onion

15 oz/425 g canned or bottled
Italian-style tomato sauce

1/2 cup/4 fl oz/125 ml dry white
or red wine

2 tablespoons chopped
parsley

1 teaspoon dried Italian
seasoning, crushed

1/2 teaspoon salt

1/4 teaspoon pepper

8 oz/250 g rigatoni
or penne

Preparation Time 15 minutes
Cooking Time 45 to 50 minutes
Serves 4 as a main course

Not fancy, but eminently satisfying: sausage, mushrooms, wine, and onions bound together in a hearty tomato sauce.

In a large frying pan cook sausage, mushrooms, and onion for 5 minutes, or till sausage is brown and onion and mushrooms are tender. Drain off fat. Add the tomato sauce, wine, parsley, Italian seasoning, salt, and pepper. Bring to boiling; reduce heat. Cover and simmer for 30 minutes. Uncover and simmer for 10 to 15 minutes more, or to desired consistency, stirring occasionally.

Meanwhile, in a large saucepan or pasta pot bring 12 cups/3 qt/3 l water to boiling. Add pasta. Reduce heat slightly. Boil, uncovered, for 14 to 15 minutes, or till al dente, stirring occasionally. (Or, cook according to package directions.) Drain, then pour sauce over hot cooked pasta and serve.

Per serving 566 calories/2,377 kilojoules, 27 g protein, 57 g carbohydrate, 23 g total fat (8 g saturated), 66 mg cholesterol, 1,713 mg sodium, 822 mg potassium

Baked Pasta & Cheddar with Ham

Chopped carrots and peppers add a festive sprinkling of color to this cheerful and easy casserole. It's a meal in itself served with steamed vegetables.

INGREDIENTS

8 oz/250 g tricolored or plain rotini or other dried shaped pasta

1 medium carrot, cut into thin, bite-size strips

1 oz/30 g chopped onion

2 oz/60 g margarine or butter

1/3 cup/1 1/2 oz/45 g all-purpose (plain) flour

1/4 teaspoon pepper

3 cups/24 fl oz/750 ml milk

1 1/4 cups/5 oz/155 g shredded Cheddar cheese

2 1/2 oz/75 g chopped green pepper (capsicum)

2 1/2 oz/75 g chopped red pepper (capsicum)

2 cups/12 oz/375 g chopped cooked ham

1/4 cup/1 oz/30 g shredded Cheddar cheese

pepper (optional)

Preparation Time 30 minutes
Baking Time 30 minutes
Serves 6 as a main course

With the addition of chopped ham and vegetables, baked macaroni and cheese expands to a full-course meal that will satisfy everyone, young and old.

METHOD FOR MAKING BAKED PASTA & CHEDDAR WITH HAM

STEPS AT A GLANCE   Page
■ Cooking pasta   22–27

In a large saucepan or pasta pot bring 12 cups/3 qt/3 l water to boiling. Add pasta. Reduce heat slightly. Boil, uncovered, for 8 to 10 minutes, or till pasta is al dente, stirring occasionally. Add carrot to boiling pasta during the last 2 minutes of cooking. (Or, cook according to package directions, adding carrot for the last 2 minutes.) Drain immediately.

Meanwhile, in a large saucepan cook onion in margarine or butter for 5 minutes, or till tender but not brown. Stir in flour and pepper. Add milk all at once. Cook and stir till slightly thickened and bubbly. Add 1¼ cups/5 oz/155 g Cheddar cheese; stir till melted. Stir in pasta-carrot mixture, green and red pepper, and ham.

Transfer mixture to a 8-cup/2-qt/2-l round casserole. Bake, covered, in a preheated 350°F/180°C/Gas Mark 4 oven for 25 minutes. Remove from oven and sprinkle with ¼ cup/1 oz/30 g Cheddar cheese and pepper, if desired. Return to oven and bake, uncovered, for 5 minutes more.

Per serving 476 calories/2,000 kilojoules, 26 g protein, 44 g carbohydrate, 21 g total fat (9 g saturated), 48 mg cholesterol, 933 mg sodium, 495 mg potassium

Neapolitan Sauce with Penne

A tiny dash of anchovy paste helps give the sauce for this pasta dish the inimitable flavor of Southern Italian cooking.

INGREDIENTS

1½ oz/45 g finely chopped onion

2 cloves garlic, minced

1 tablespoon olive oil or cooking oil

28 oz/875 g canned whole Italian-style tomatoes, cut up

2 tablespoons chopped fresh oregano or 2 teaspoons dried oregano, crushed

2 tablespoons tomato paste

1 tablespoon capers, drained and rinsed

1 teaspoon sugar

1 teaspoon anchovy paste

⅛ to ¼ teaspoon ground red pepper (cayenne)

6 oz/185 g penne, rigatoni, or other dried shaped pasta

1½ oz/45 g kalamata olives, pitted and chopped, or pitted black olives, chopped

2 tablespoons chopped fresh parsley

Preparation Time 15 minutes
Cooking Time 20 minutes
Serves 6 as an accompaniment or first course

Unmistakably Italian, this sauce contains capers, anchovies, ripe olives, and other Mediterranean flavors.

METHOD FOR MAKING NEAPOLITAN SAUCE WITH PENNE

In a large saucepan cook the onion and garlic in hot oil till onion is tender but not brown. Stir in the undrained tomatoes, oregano, tomato paste, capers, sugar, anchovy paste, and red pepper. Bring to boiling; reduce heat. Simmer, uncovered, for about 20 minutes, or to desired consistency.

Meanwhile, in a large saucepan or pasta pot bring 12 cups/3 qt/3 l water to boiling. Add pasta. Reduce heat slightly. Boil, uncovered, 14 to 15 minutes, or till al dente, stirring occasionally. (Or, cook according to package directions.) Drain immediately. Return pasta to the pan.

Pour tomato mixture and olives over hot cooked pasta and toss to coat pasta. Transfer to a warm serving dish. Sprinkle with parsley and serve immediately.

Per serving 179 calories/752 kilojoules, 6 g protein, 31 g carbohydrate, 4 g total fat (1 g saturated), 1 mg cholesterol, 304 mg sodium, 414 mg potassium

Shaped Pasta

Broccoli & Pasta in Garlic Butter

Combine crisp florets of broccoli or cauliflower with little pasta wheels for an easy but delicious side dish that contrasts crisp and al dente textures. Another time, try the hybrid broccoflower, also known as broccolo Romano.

INGREDIENTS

4 oz/125 g ruote, conchiglie or other dried shaped pasta

4 oz/125 g broccoli or cauliflower florets

1 tablespoon chopped fresh basil or 1/2 teaspoon dried basil, crushed

2 cloves garlic, halved lengthwise

2 tablespoons margarine or butter

2 tablespoons olive oil or cooking oil

1/4 cup/1 oz/30 g grated Romano or Parmesan cheese

pepper (optional)

Preparation Time 15 minutes
Cooking Time 12 to 14 minutes
Serves 4 as an accompaniment or first course

A simple sauce of butter, olive oil, garlic, and broccoli is tossed with ruote (wagon-wheel pasta).

METHOD FOR MAKING BROCCOLI & PASTA IN GARLIC BUTTER

In a large saucepan or pasta pot bring 12 cups/3 qt/3 l water to boiling. Add pasta. Reduce heat slightly. Boil, uncovered, for 12 to 14 minutes, or till al dente, stirring occasionally. (Or, cook according to package directions.) Drain immediately.

Meanwhile, in a medium saucepan cook broccoli or cauliflower florets and basil, covered, in a small amount of boiling salted water for 6 to 8 minutes or till crisp-tender. Drain well. In a large frying pan cook the garlic in hot margarine or butter and olive oil or cooking oil for about 5 minutes, or till garlic is golden, stirring occasionally. Remove garlic from pan and discard.

Add broccoli or cauliflower florets to warm pan and toss to coat with margarine-oil mixture; heat through. Add hot cooked pasta and Romano or Parmesan cheese and toss to mix. Transfer to a warm serving dish. If desired, sprinkle with pepper. Serve immediately.

Per serving 271 calories/1,138 kilojoules, 8 g protein, 27 g carbohydrate, 15 g total fat (3 g saturated), 7 mg cholesterol, 173 mg sodium, 269 mg potassium

White Cheese & Macaroni

The pasta can be cooked ahead, if you prefer. Drain, toss in a little oil, cover, and set aside for up to 2 hours or until needed. When preparing the sauce, return the cooked pasta to the saucepan, add the remaining ingredients, and finish the recipe as directed.

INGREDIENTS

4 oz/125 g elbow macaroni or ditalini

1 large clove garlic, cut lengthwise into slivers

1/3 cup/3 fl oz/80 ml milk

1 tablespoon margarine or butter

1 cup/4 oz/125 g shredded sharp white Cheddar cheese

1/4 teaspoon white or black pepper

1 tablespoon chopped fresh parsley

Preparation Time 15 minutes
Cooking Time 10 to 13 minutes
Serves 4 as an accompaniment or first course

STEPS AT A GLANCE	Page
▨ Cooking pasta	22–27

Sharp white Cheddar cheese and slivers of garlic transform a childhood favorite into a grown-up accompaniment for grilled fish or meat.

METHOD FOR MAKING WHITE CHEESE & MACARONI

In a large saucepan or pasta pot bring 12 cups/3 qt/3 l water to boiling. Add pasta and garlic slivers. Reduce heat slightly. Boil, uncovered, for 8 to 10 minutes, or till al dente, stirring occasionally. (Or, cook according to package directions.) Drain immediately.

Return pasta and garlic to warm pan. Add milk. Cook on low heat for 2 to 3 minutes, or till all the milk is absorbed by the pasta. Add margarine or butter, cheese, and pepper. Stir mixture gently till cheese is melted. Garnish with parsley and serve.

Per serving 275 calories/1,155 kilojoules, 12 g protein, 27 g carbohydrate, 13 g total fat (7 g saturated), 31 mg cholesterol, 221 mg sodium, 97 mg potassium

LAYERED PASTA

Making Layered Pasta

Lasagne, made with packaged noodles, cheese, and tomato-meat sauce, is probably the most familiar layered pasta, but by no means the only one, as you will discover in this chapter. The steps and recipes that follow clearly demonstrate that layered pasta is a whole category of tempting recipes, not just a single dish.

The ingredients make the difference; the technique varies only slightly. Each is a construction of pasta and filling, with every layer contrasting yet complementing the others. Each is assembled in an ovenproof dish and baked until piping hot from top to bottom. All are hearty, satisfying, and good for casual party meals because they can be prepared in advance and reheated.

Lasagne Verdi, page 225, is a classic dish made with fresh or dried spinach noodles. Salmon Lasagne with Roasted Pepper Sauce, page 208, is a contemporary seafood casserole, and Vegetable Lasagne, page 219, dispenses with meat altogether to show off a cornucopia of vegetables. Some recipes use shaped pasta rather than flat sheets: Four Seasons Pasta Pie, page 205, has a spaghetti "crust," while both Greek-inspired Pastitsio, page 212, and Spicy Turkey & Corn Pasta, page 222, include macaroni.

Equipment for preparing and serving layered pasta casseroles includes a chef's knife, assorted bowls, and spatulas. A pastry wheel and ruler are helpful when cutting fresh lasagne noodles.

baking dish

cutting board and glass bowls

chef's knife

fluted pastry wheel

ruler

large, wide spatula

metal spatula

dried pasta may be substituted for fresh pasta in layered dishes

STEP 1

Cutting Fresh Lasagne Noodles
Let the rolled fresh dough rest for about 20 minutes to dry slightly. Trim each piece to a large rectangle, as specified in the recipe. With a fluted pastry wheel or a sharp knife, cut each rectangle into even strips, using a ruler as a guide.

fresh noodles need only to be cooked briefly before layering

STEP 2

Setting the Noodles Aside
If necessary, trim the strips further to the size specified in the recipe. Place the strips on slightly damp kitchen towels so they won't dry out while you are cutting the remaining rectangles of dough. After cooking the noodles, place them on the towels to keep them from sticking together.

you can also use a rubber spatula or wooden spoon to spread the cheese or filling

STEP 3

Assembling the Dish
Cover the bottom of the dish with a little sauce to keep the noodles from sticking to the dish. Top with noodles, more sauce, and grated cheeses. Add the next layer of noodles. With a metal spatula, spread ricotta cheese or filling evenly across the noodles.

vary the recipe by using other kinds of shredded cheeses

STEP 4

Sprinkling with Cheese
Arrange a layer of noodles over the filling. Spoon on the remaining sauce and spread to cover the pasta. Finish layering by sprinkling with the remaining cheeses.

the casserole will cut more easily if allowed to rest first to let the layers cool and set

STEP 5

Cutting into Servings
Remove lasagne from the oven and let sit for 10 minutes. Cut into serving-size portions with a sharp knife. Transfer each portion to individual plates with a large, wide spatula.

Layers of fresh spinach pasta alternate with creamy cheeses and a rich meat sauce to make hearty Lasagne Verdi (page 225).

This savory pie has a spaghetti "crust", a peppery cheese filling, and a topping of pesto, prosciutto or ham, mushrooms, and tomatoes.

Four Seasons Pasta Pie

If fresh plum tomatoes aren't in season, peel and thinly slice 1 large tomato, then cut the slices in half and arrange on top of the prosciutto or ham.

INGREDIENTS

CRUST

5 oz/155 g dried spaghetti or linguine or 10 oz/315 g fresh linguine

1 beaten egg

1/4 cup/1 oz/30 g grated Parmesan cheese

1 tablespoon margarine or butter

CHEESE FILLING

1 beaten egg

1 cup/8 oz/250 g ricotta cheese

1/8 teaspoon pepper

TOPPING

1 1/2 oz/45 g sliced fresh mushrooms

1 teaspoon olive oil

1 oz/30 g prosciutto or cooked ham, chopped

2 plum (Roma) tomatoes, thinly sliced

4 teaspoons pesto (page 49)

2 tablespoons grated Parmesan cheese

METHOD FOR MAKING FOUR SEASONS PASTA PIE

Preparation Time 30 minutes
Baking Time 25 minutes
Serves 4 as a main course

STEPS AT A GLANCE	Page
■ Cooking pasta	22–27
■ Making pesto	49
■ Making pasta pie	207

For crust, bring 12 cups/3 qt/3 l water to boiling in a pasta pot or large saucepan. Add pasta. Reduce heat slightly. Boil, stirring occasionally, uncovered, for 8 to 12 minutes for dried pasta or 1½ to 2 minutes for fresh, or till al dente. (Or, cook according to package directions.) Drain immediately. Return to warm pan.

Meanwhile, in a medium mixing bowl combine egg, Parmesan cheese, and margarine or butter. Pour over hot spaghetti in saucepan and toss to coat. Press spaghetti mixture evenly into bottom and up sides of a well-greased 9-in/23-cm pie plate.

For cheese filling, in a small mixing bowl combine egg, ricotta cheese, and pepper. Spread over spaghetti crust.

For topping, in a medium frying pan cook and stir mushrooms in hot oil for 2 minutes, or till tender. Set aside. Sprinkle chopped prosciutto or ham over cheese filling. Arrange tomato slices in a circle 1 in/2.5 cm

from the edge of the pie plate. Dot pesto on tomato slices. Arrange mushrooms inside the circle of tomatoes.

Cover and bake in a preheated 350°F/180°C/Gas Mark 4 oven for 20 minutes. Uncover and sprinkle with Parmesan cheese. Bake, uncovered, for about 5 minutes more, or till cheese melts. Let stand for 5 to 10 minutes before serving. Cut into wedges to serve.

Per serving 513 calories/2,154 kilojoules, 27 g protein, 53 g carbohydrate, 21 g total fat (7 g saturated), 195 mg cholesterol, 495 mg sodium, 282 mg potassium

STEP 1

Forming the Crust

With the back of a wooden spoon, press the spaghetti-egg mixture against the bottom and sides of a well-greased 9-in/23-cm pie plate.

STEP 2

Dotting with Pesto

Spread the ricotta cheese mixture over the crust and top with the prosciutto or ham and tomatoes. Scoop up the pesto with a small spoon and push it off with a small spatula onto the tomatoes. Top with a ring of sautéed sliced mushrooms.

Salmon Lasagne with Roasted Pepper Sauce

To use fresh lasagne noodles for this dish, follow the directions in the recipe on page 225, using 3 portions homemade pasta to make 9 noodles.

INGREDIENTS

12 oz/375 g skinless fresh or frozen salmon fillets or
12 oz/375 g canned boneless, skinless salmon, drained and broken up

2 large red peppers (capsicums)

1/3 cup/3 fl oz/80 ml pesto (page 49)

9 dried lasagne noodles

1/2 cup/4 fl oz/125 ml sour cream

1 tablespoon all-purpose (plain) flour

1/4 teaspoon salt

1/8 teaspoon pepper

1 beaten egg

1 cup/8 oz/250 g ricotta cheese

1 cup/8 oz/250 g packaged cream cheese, softened

Preparation Time 1½ hours
Baking Time 30 to 35 minutes
Serves 8 as a main course

Roasted peppers delicately tint and flavor the top layer of a seafood-and-pesto lasagne.

Thaw salmon, if frozen. Halve red peppers; remove stems, seeds, and membranes. Place peppers, cut-side down, on a foil-lined baking sheet. Bake in a preheated 425°F/210°C/Gas Mark 5 oven for 20 to 25 minutes, or till skins are blistered and dark. Remove from baking sheet. Immediately place in a paper bag. Close bag; let stand about 30 minutes to steam so skins peel away more easily.

(Or, place bag in freezer for 5 to 10 minutes.) With a sharp knife, remove skin from peppers, pulling it off in strips. Discard skins. Reduce oven temperature to 375°F/190°C/ Gas Mark 4.

Meanwhile, prepare pesto as directed. Set aside. If using fresh or thawed frozen salmon fillets, bring about 1½ cups/12 fl oz/ 375 ml water to boiling in a large frying pan. Measure the thickness of salmon fillets. Add salmon to pan. Return just to boiling and reduce heat. Cover and simmer for 4 to 6 minutes per ½-in/12-mm thickness. Drain, discarding cooking liquid. Use a fork to break fish carefully into bite-size pieces, discarding soft bones. Set aside.

In a large saucepan or pasta pot bring 12 cups/3 qt/3 l water to boiling. Add pasta. Reduce heat slightly. Boil, uncovered, for 10 to 12 minutes, or till al dente, stirring occasionally. (Or, cook according to package directions.) Drain immediately. Rinse with cold water; drain.

In a food processor bowl or blender container, process or blend the roasted peppers till nearly smooth. Add sour cream, flour, salt, and pepper. Process or blend till combined and smooth. Set aside.

In a medium mixing bowl combine egg, ricotta cheese, and cream cheese. Stir in pesto and cooked or canned salmon.

To assemble, lightly grease an 8-cup/2-qt/2-l rectangular baking dish. Arrange 3 of the noodles in the bottom of the dish. Spread with one-third of the cheese mixture. Repeat layers twice. Carefully spread roasted red pepper mixture over the top layer.

Bake, uncovered, in a 375°F/190°C/Gas Mark 4 oven for 30 to 35 minutes, or till heated through. Let stand for 10 minutes before serving.

Per serving 386 calories/1,621 kilojoules, 17 g protein, 24 g carbohydrate, 25 g total fat (10 g saturated), 83 mg cholesterol, 309 mg sodium, 209 mg potassium

STEP 1

Roasting Peppers
Place stemmed and seeded pepper halves on a foil-lined baking sheet. Roast in a preheated 425°F/210°C/Gas Mark 5 oven until the skins are blistered.

STEP 2

Peeling Peppers
After cooling the peppers, peel away the skin by pulling it off in strips with a sharp paring knife.

A simple vegetable accompaniment such as grilled eggplant (aubergine) and fresh tomato will go nicely with this traditional Greek pasta casserole.

Pastitsio

The white sauce firms up into a creamy, delicious layer, and the cinnamon adds an exotic flavor to this traditional Greek dish.

INGREDIENTS

meat sauce (page 119)

PASTA

8 oz/250 g elbow macaroni

1 beaten egg

1/4 cup/1 oz/30 g grated
Parmesan cheese

Preparation Time 45 minutes
(includes sauce)
Baking Time 30 to 35 minutes
Serves 6 as a main course

WHITE SAUCE

3 tablespoons margarine
or butter

3 tablespoons all-purpose
(plain) flour

1/4 teaspoon pepper

1 1/2 cups/12 fl oz/375 ml milk

1 beaten egg

1/4 cup/1 oz/30 g grated
Parmesan cheese

ground cinnamon (optional)

METHOD FOR MAKING PASTITSIO

Per serving 429 calories/1,802 kilojoules, 26 g protein, 45 g carbohydrate, 16 g total fat (5 g saturated), 118 mg cholesterol, 672 mg sodium, 660 mg potassium

Prepare the meat sauce as directed. Set aside.

For pasta, in a large saucepan or pasta pot bring 12 cups/3 qt/3 l water to boiling. Add pasta. Reduce heat slightly. Boil, uncovered, for about 10 minutes, or till al dente, stirring occasionally. (Or, cook according to package directions.) Drain immediately. Rinse with cold water. Drain again.

In a large mixing bowl combine 1 beaten egg, ¼ cup/1 oz/30 g Parmesan cheese, and cooked macaroni. Set aside.

For white sauce, in a medium saucepan melt margarine or butter. Stir in flour and pepper. Add the milk all at once. Cook and stir till smooth, thickened and bubbly. Stir about half the mixture into 1 beaten egg. Return egg mixture to the saucepan. Stir in ¼ cup/ 1 oz/30 g Parmesan cheese.

To assemble, layer half of the pasta mixture in a greased 8-cup/ 2-qt/2-l square baking dish. Top with all the meat sauce, the remaining pasta mixture, and all the white sauce. If desired, sprinkle lightly with cinnamon.

Bake in a preheated 350°F/180°C/Gas Mark 4 oven for 30 to 35 minutes, or till set. Let stand for 5 minutes before serving.

STEP 1

Making Pasta Mixture

Cook the macaroni, then drain thoroughly. In a large mixing bowl, combine the pasta with the egg and grated Parmesan cheese. Mix well.

STEP 2

Layering

Spread half the pasta mixture on the bottom of an 8-cup/2-qt/2-l baking dish. Cover with the meat sauce. Then, spoon on the remaining pasta so that it covers the sauce completely. Top with all the white sauce.

Baked Eggplant, Tomato & Pasta Gratin

This rustic dish combines some of the intense flavors of southern Italy: tomatoes, eggplant and mozzarella cheese.

INGREDIENTS

3 medium eggplants (aubergines)

1/3 cup/2 1/2 fl oz/80 ml olive oil

2 onions, chopped

2 cloves garlic, chopped

14 oz/440 g canned whole Italian-style tomatoes, chopped

2 tablespoons tomato paste

2 teaspoons dried basil

1 teaspoon dried oregano

1/2 teaspoon salt

1/8 teaspoon black pepper

8 oz/250 g penne or other dried shaped pasta

10 oz/315 g mozzarella cheese, sliced

Preparation Time 35 minutes
Cooking Time 1 1/4 hours
Serves 6

STEPS AT A GLANCE   Page

Cooking pasta   **22–27**

Cutting up canned tomatoes **37**

The eggplants are fried in olive oil then layered with pasta in tomato sauce, and slices of mozzarella cheese.

Cut the eggplants crosswise into thin slices. Arrange in a colander and sprinkle with salt. Let stand for about 30 minutes to release the bitter juices. Rinse under cold running water. Pat dry with paper towels.

Heat half the olive oil in a large saucepan. Add the onion and garlic and cook till tender. Add the undrained tomatoes, tomato paste, basil and oregano and bring to boiling. Simmer for 30 minutes, or until well thickened. Add salt and pepper.

In a large frying pan, heat the remaining olive oil. Working in batches, fry the eggplant slices on both sides until cooked through and lightly golden. Add more oil as necessary. Drain the eggplant slices on paper towels.

In a large saucepan or pasta pot bring 12 cups/ 3 qt/3 l water to boiling. Add pasta. Reduce heat slightly. Boil, stirring occasionally, uncovered, for 14 to 15 minutes, or until al dente. (Or, follow package directions.) Drain, add to tomato sauce.

To assemble, grease an 8-cup/2 qt/2 l baking dish. Arrange the ingredients in the dish in the following sequence: one-third eggplant slices, half tomato pasta sauce, one-third eggplant slices, half mozzarella slices, half tomato pasta sauce, one-third eggplant slices, half mozzarella slices.

Bake, uncovered, in a preheated 350°F/180°C/Gas Mark 4 oven for 30 minutes, or until the cheese on top is melted and golden.

Per serving 515 calories/2,163 kilojoules, 23 g protein, 41 g carbohydrate, 30 g total fat (10 g saturated), 33 mg cholesterol, 438 mg sodium, 791 mg potassium

Vegetable Lasagne

To prepare this dish with fresh lasagne noodles, follow the directions in the recipe on page 225, using 2 portions of homemade pasta. If you want to use fresh artichoke hearts, prepare them as directed on page 153, then boil them for about 5 minutes.

INGREDIENTS

6 dried lasagne noodles

VEGETABLES

9 oz/280 g package frozen artichoke hearts

8 oz/250 g sliced fresh mushrooms

1 cup/5 oz/155 g shredded carrot

1 tablespoon margarine or butter

SAUCE

1 1/2 oz/45 g sliced scallions (spring onions)

2 cloves garlic, minced

1 tablespoon margarine or butter

1/4 cup/1 oz/30 g all-purpose (plain) flour

1/4 teaspoon pepper

1 cup/8 fl oz/250 ml light (single) cream or milk

3/4 cup/6 fl oz/185 ml chicken stock

FILLING

10 oz/315 g frozen chopped spinach, thawed and drained

1 cup/8 oz/250 g cream-style cottage cheese, drained

1/4 cup/1 oz/30 g grated Parmesan cheese

1/4 cup/1 oz/30 g grated Parmesan cheese, for topping

Preparation Time 40 minutes
Baking Time 40 to 45 minutes
Serves 8 as a main course

Chunky vegetables such as artichoke hearts, mushrooms, and carrots add appealing texture and crunch to a meatless lasagne.

In a large saucepan or pasta pot bring 12 cups/3 qt/3 l water to boiling. Add pasta. Reduce heat slightly. Boil, uncovered, for 10 to 12 minutes, or till al dente, stirring occasionally. (Or, follow package directions.) Drain immediately. Rinse with cold water; drain again.

For vegetables, cook artichoke hearts according to package directions. Drain and chop. In a large frying pan cook mushrooms and carrots in margarine or butter for 3 minutes, or till tender. Stir in chopped artichoke hearts. Set vegetable mixture aside.

For sauce, in a medium saucepan cook scallion and garlic in hot margarine or butter till tender. Stir in flour and pepper. Add light cream or milk and chicken stock all at once. Cook and stir till thickened and bubbly. Remove from heat and set aside.

For filling, in a medium mixing bowl combine spinach, cottage cheese, and Parmesan cheese.

To assemble, grease an 8-cup/ 2-qt/2-l rectangular baking dish. Arrange 3 noodles in the prepared dish. Spread half of the filling on top of the noodles. Spoon half the vegetable mixture over the filling. Spoon half the sauce over top. Repeat layers.

Bake, covered, in a preheated 350°F/180°C/Gas Mark 4 oven for 35 minutes. Uncover and sprinkle ¼ cup/1 oz/30 g Parmesan cheese over the top. Bake for 5 to 10 minutes more, or till mixture is heated through. Let stand for 10 minutes before serving.

Per serving 233 calories/978 kilojoules, 13 g protein, 26 g carbohydrate, 10 g total fat (4 g saturated), 18 mg cholesterol, 415 mg sodium, 471 mg potassium

Spicy Turkey & Corn Pasta

If you like Mexican food, here's a one-course meal chock-full of all your favorite
Mexican spices. Look for the corn elbow macaroni at health food shops;
it is often used by people on wheat-free diets.

INGREDIENTS

12 oz/375 g ground (minced),
uncooked turkey meat

2 oz/60 g chopped onion

1 clove garlic, minced

15 oz/425 g canned or bottled
Italian-style tomato sauce

1 cup/8 fl oz/250 ml water

2 tablespoons chopped cilantro
(fresh coriander) (optional)

1 tablespoon tomato paste

1/2 teaspoon salt

1/2 teaspoon ground cumin

1/4 teaspoon chili powder

1/4 teaspoon ground coriander

1/8 teaspoon ground red pepper
(cayenne)

4 oz/125 g corn or plain elbow
macaroni

8 oz/250 g canned red kidney
beans, drained

1 cup/4 oz/125 g shredded
provolone cheese

A fruit garnish of juicy orange wedges and tart-sweet kiwi fruit helps to cool the fire of a spicy Mexican pasta main course.

Preparation Time 30 minutes
Baking Time 30 to 45 minutes
Serves 6 as a main course

In a large frying pan cook the turkey, onion, and garlic for 5 minutes, or till meat is brown. Drain off fat. Add tomato sauce, water, cilantro leaves (if desired), tomato paste, salt, cumin, chili powder, ground coriander, and red pepper. Bring to boiling; reduce heat. Cover and simmer for 15 minutes.

Lightly grease an 8-cup/2-qt/2-l square baking dish. Layer half the uncooked elbow macaroni, half the turkey mixture, half the beans, and half the cheese. Repeat layers.

Bake, covered, in a preheated 350°F/180°C/Gas Mark 4 oven for 20 minutes (40 minutes for plain macaroni). Uncover and bake for 10 minutes more (5 minutes more for plain macaroni), or till pasta is tender and mixture is heated through. Let stand for 10 minutes before serving.

Per serving 327 calories/1,373 kilojoules, 19 g protein, 26 g carbohydrate, 18 g total fat (4 g saturated), 17 mg cholesterol, 826 mg sodium, 403 mg potassium

Lasagne Verdi

In Italian, verdi means "green," and green spinach pasta is what gives
this recipe its name. You can use plain pasta if you prefer.

INGREDIENTS

9 dried spinach or plain lasagne
noodles or 3 portions
homemade pasta (page 28)

Bolognese sauce (page 44)

2 tablespoons margarine or
butter

2 tablespoons all-purpose
(plain) flour

¹/₄ teaspoon salt

dash of pepper

²/₃ cup/5 fl oz/160 ml milk

¹/₂ cup/4 oz/125 g ricotta cheese

2 cups/8 oz/250 g shredded
mozzarella cheese

¹/₄ cup/1 oz/30 g
grated Parmesan
cheese

Preparation Time 1¹/₄ hours
(includes sauce)
Baking Time 30 minutes
Serves 6 to 8 as a main course

This appealing lasagne displays all the colors of the Italian flag: green spinach noodles, creamy white cheese, and tomato-red sauce.

METHOD FOR MAKING LASAGNE VERDI

If using homemade pasta, roll each portion of dough to a 12x9-in/30x23-cm rectangle. Cut into three noodles, each measuring 12x22-in/30x6-cm.

Prepare Bolognese sauce, except omit the cream and nutmeg. Set aside. In a small saucepan melt margarine or butter. Stir in flour, salt, and pepper. Add milk all at once. Cook and stir over medium heat till thickened and bubbly. Stir in ricotta cheese.

In a large saucepan or pasta pot bring 12 cups/3 qt/3 l water to boiling. Add pasta. Reduce heat slightly. Boil, uncovered, for 10 to 12 minutes for dried pasta or 2 to 3 minutes for fresh, or till al dente, stirring occasionally. (Or, cook according to package directions.) Drain immediately. Rinse with cold water and drain again.

Spread ½ cup/4 fl oz/125 ml of the Bolognese sauce in the bottom of a greased 8-cup/2-qt/2-l rectangular baking dish. Arrange one-third of the noodles on top of the sauce. Spread with half the remaining Bolognese sauce. Sprinkle with half the mozzarella and half the

Parmesan. Add another layer of noodles and all the ricotta mixture. Repeat layers with remaining noodles, Bolognese sauce, mozzarella, and Parmesan. Bake, uncovered, in a preheated 375°F/190°C/Gas Mark 4 oven for 30 minutes, or till heated through. Let stand for 10 minutes before serving.

Per serving 534 calories/2,243 kilojoules, 33 g protein, 47 g carbohydrate, 23 g total fat (10 g saturated), 70 mg cholesterol, 732 mg sodium, 878 mg potassium

STUFFED PASTA

A ravioli frame allows for assembly-line efficiency when filling, sealing, and scoring pasta squares, but it is almost as easy to shape them by hand and cut them with a pastry wheel. Bowls and a measuring spoon are also necessary for stuffing pasta, and a small paintbrush is helpful for sealing.

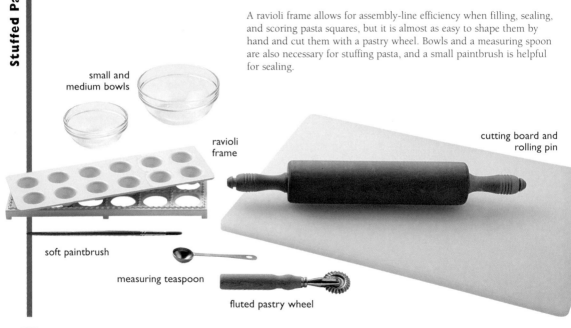

small and medium bowls

ravioli frame

cutting board and rolling pin

soft paintbrush

measuring teaspoon

fluted pastry wheel

Stuffing Pasta

Although delicate and tender, fresh pasta is sturdy enough to serve as edible wrapping for all sorts of tasty bundles. Some enclose the filling completely so that the first bite is a delicious surprise. These include square ravioli, half-moon-shaped agnolotti, and ring-shaped tortellini. Tubular cannelloni and manicotti — discussed on pages 236 to 241— and their close kin the pasta roll (see Stuffed Pasta Rolls, page 243), are left partially open to reveal some of the savory mixture encased within.

Classic fillings incorporate cheeses like creamy ricotta and pungent grated Parmesan, and chopped spinach or ham, all bound with a little egg. Others feature meaty mushrooms, spicy sausage seasoned with herbs, or intensely tasty dried tomatoes. These pastas and fillings nicely mix and match, so you can experiment and interchange them for variety.

Regardless of their final form, all these packages begin with a basic pasta dough rolled by hand or with a machine into thin sheets as for lasagne or ribbon pasta. To review this technique, see Steps for Making Pasta, pages 12 to 31. Unlike ribbon pasta, however, pasta for stuffing must be pliable. Don't let the rolled sheet dry or you won't be able to shape it. Use immediately and cover unused portions with a kitchen towel or plastic wrap until needed.

Shape and fill ravioli and tortellini one step at a time. Always leave a sufficient margin of dough around the filling to ensure a good seal. For a different look, vary the size by using large, wide strips for ravioli or bigger circles for tortellini. A trio or quartet of 3-in/7.5-cm ravioli looks quite dramatic as a first course. Create an attractive edge on either ravioli or tortellini by cutting with a fluted pastry wheel or scalloped cutter.

Forming ravioli by hand is very easy, but a metal frame already molded with indentations and scoring notches will speed the process up. Most kitchenware shops or larger store kitchenware departments stock these. Both hand and frame methods for ravioli are shown in steps 1 to 4 on pages 233 to 234. Forming the little half-moon shapes of tortellini is shown in steps 5 and 6 on page 235.

Stuffed pasta can be made early in the day and cooked close to serving time. Arrange on a flour-dusted tray, lightly dust with a little more flour, and refrigerate, covered with a kitchen towel. Don't let the pieces touch or they might stick together and tear when you try to separate them.

press out as much
air as possible
around filling
before sealing

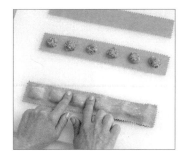

STEP 1

Sealing Ravioli

On each 2x12-in/5x30-cm strip of dough, arrange
1 teaspoon of filling every 2 in/5 cm, beginning
1 in/2.5 cm from one end. Moisten the dough around
the filling with a small paintbrush or your finger, top
with another strip of dough and press down on either
side of the filling to seal.

press down the
edges of the cut
ravioli one more
time to seal

STEP 2

Cutting Ravioli

With a fluted pastry cutter or sharp knife, cut halfway
between the mounds of filling to separate the ravioli.
Repeat with the remaining pasta and filling.

about one teaspoonful is the correct amount of filling

STEP 3

Making Ravioli with a Frame

Drape a sheet of fresh dough on the bottom of the frame. Press lightly into each hollow, or set the top of the frame (if there is one) on the dough and press gently. Place about 1 teaspoon of filling in each hollow.

after sealing, remove the ravioli from the frame and pull them apart at the seams

STEP 4

Sealing Ravioli in a Frame

Brush the dough lightly with water. Set another rectangle of dough on top of the filling. Using firm, even pressure, push a wooden rolling pin across. Or, apply the top of the frame, if there is one. This action both seals the ravioli and scores them.

you can work
faster if you fill a
number of circles
at one time

STEP 5

Folding Tortellini

Stamp out little rounds of dough with a 1½ in/4-cm round cutter. Place about 4 teaspoons of filling in the center of each round. Brush the edge with water. Create a half-moon by folding the dough circle in half. Pinch along the edge to seal.

if the dough has
dried out, moisten
the ends before
you pinch them
together

STEP 6

Shaping Tortellini

Bend the half-moon, seam-side out, and bring the two outer ends together. Pinch them to seal. For larger tortellini, shape by placing a finger against the fold and bending around it; overlap the ends and pinch.

Stuffing Manicotti and Cannelloni

Manicotti and cannelloni are luscious rolls of pasta wrapped around cheese, meat, and vegetables. Both are easily assembled using paper-thin squares or rectangles of fresh dough or dried pasta tubes. The two are essentially the same dish with one difference: manicotti are rolled on the diagonal, while cannelloni are rolled straight across. As seems to be true with all Italian pasta, even such a slight variation is inspiration for an entirely new name.

Both fresh pasta squares or rectangles and dried pasta tubes must be cooked in boiling water until just al dente. Don't overcook or overstuff dried pasta tubes, or they will burst as they expand during baking. For a more attractive shape, always roll cooked fresh pasta in a tight bundle around the filling.

Classic Cannelloni, on page 275, is filled with a creamy chicken mixture and topped with tomato and cheese sauces side by side. The chicken filling can be replaced by Bolognese sauce (page 44) if you prefer. Grilled Spinach Cannelloni, page 272, is quickly browned under the grill and covered with a lemony cream sauce. Manicotti with Roasted Vegetables, page 269, is baked with fresh tomato sauce and a topping of garlic-infused vegetables.

BASIC TOOLS FOR STUFFING MANICOTTI AND CANNELLONI

A ruler and rolling cutter make quick work of dividing pasta sheets into uniform squares or rectangles. Use a small spoon to fill cooked tubes so that their delicate walls won't tear. An ovenproof baking dish holds the finished product.

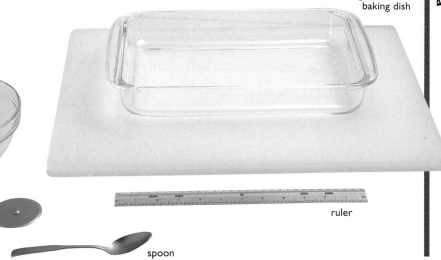

cutting board and baking dish

bowl

pizza cutter

ruler

spoon

to make straight
cuts, use a ruler
as a guide

STEP 1

Cutting Pasta Sheets

Roll pasta into a thin sheet. Cut the sheet of dough into
squares or rectangles, as directed in the recipe. Use a
pizza cutter, a fluted pastry wheel, or a sharp knife.

use gentle
pressure when
rolling so the
filling isn't
squeezed out

STEP 2

Filling Cannelloni

Cook the pasta squares or rectangles until al dente. Drain
and place on a kitchen towel. Spoon the filling along one
edge of each cooked pasta piece. Roll the dough tightly
around the filling.

fill from the center to the open end, then turn and fill the other end

STEP 3

Filling Dried Manicotti

Cook the shells until al dente. Drain and place on a kitchen towel. With a small spoon, carefully insert equal amounts of filling into each shell; do not pack filling. Take your time; the cooked manicotti shells tear easily, and must be handled gently.

some of the filling will be exposed at either end

STEP 4

Filling Fresh Manicotti
Cook the pasta rectangles until al dente. Drain and place on a kitchen towel. Place rectangles with one corner toward you. Spoon equal amounts of filling diagonally across and just below the center of each rectangle. Beginning at the bottom corner, roll the dough around the filling. If necessary, moisten the top corner with water to help it stick.

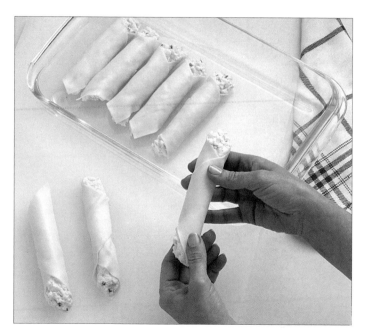

set them seam-side down so they
won't unroll

STEP 5

Placing Seam-side Down
Carefully transfer filled cannelloni
or manicotti to a baking dish.
Arrange rolled pasta in the dish with
the seams on the bottom. Leave a
space between each cannelloni or
manicotti so they will cook evenly.

Colorful pinwheels of spinach pasta and filling make a stunning presentation.

Stuffed Pasta Rolls

Pasta rolls are impressive to serve and surprisingly simple to make. When sliced, these reveal spirals of green pasta and a filling of ham, cheese, and chewy dried tomatoes. The rolls may be prepared 1 day ahead and refrigerated until ready to bake.

INGREDIENTS

1 portion (4 oz/125 g) spinach pasta (page 31)

FILLING

1/2 oz/15 g fresh chives

1/2 oz/15 g fresh parsley

1 or 2 small cloves garlic

1 cup/8 oz/250 g packaged cream cheese

1/2 cup/4 oz/125 g cream-style cottage cheese

5 oz/155 g thinly sliced prosciutto, or ham

1/2 cup/4 oz/125 g drained and finely chopped oil-packed dried tomatoes

SAUCE

6 oz/180 g sliced fresh mushrooms

2 cloves garlic, minced

3 tablespoons margarine or butter

3 tablespoons all-purpose (plain) flour

1/4 teaspoon salt

1/4 teaspoon white pepper

1 cup/8 fl oz/250 ml chicken stock

1 cup/8 fl oz/250 ml light (single) cream or milk

1/2 teaspoon finely shredded lemon peel

1 tablespoon lemon juice

Preparation Time 1½ hours
Baking Time 20 minutes
Serves 4 to 6 as a main course

Prepare spinach pasta as directed, except divide the portion of dough in half and roll each half to a 12x6-in/30x15-cm rectangle. In a large saucepan or pasta pot bring 12 cups/3 qt/3 l water to boiling. Add 1 sheet of the pasta. Reduce heat slightly. Boil, uncovered, about 3 minutes, or till pasta is al dente, stirring occasionally. Use a slotted spoon to lift pasta from water into a colander (be careful not to tear it). Rinse with cold water. Drain well. Carefully spread on a damp cloth towel. Repeat with remaining sheet.

Meanwhile, for filling, in a food processor bowl or blender container finely chop the chives, parsley, and garlic. Add cream cheese and cottage cheese and blend till nearly smooth.

To assemble, spread half the filling over each pasta sheet to within ¼ in/6 mm of the edges. Arrange the prosciutto or ham and chopped dried tomatoes in layers on top of the filling. Roll jelly-roll style, starting from one of the short sides. (If desired, cover pasta roll tightly and chill for up to 24 hours.) Trim uneven edges of rolls. Cut each roll into 6 slices. Place the slices, cut-side down, in an 8-cup/2-qt/ 2-l rectangular baking dish. Bake, covered, in a preheated 375°F/190°C/Gas Mark 4 oven for 20 minutes, or till hot.

Meanwhile, for sauce, in a medium saucepan cook mushrooms and garlic in hot margarine or butter till tender. Stir in flour, salt, and pepper. Add chicken stock and light cream or milk all at once. Cook and stir till thickened and bubbly. Cook and stir for 1 minute more. Remove from heat and stir in lemon peel and lemon juice. To serve, divide sauce among individual plates. Arrange hot pasta pinwheels on top of sauce. Serve immediately.

Per serving 520 calories/2,184 kilojoules, 25 g protein, 30 g carbohydrate, 34 g total fat (16 g saturated), 104 mg cholesterol, 1,303 mg sodium, 787 mg potassium

STEP 1

Rolling Pasta
Begin at one short end. Roll pasta and filling jelly-roll style by rolling up the towel to gently push the dough along.

STEP 3

Cutting Pasta
Trim away uneven ends of pasta rolls. Cut each roll into 6 slices with a serrated knife. Place the slices, cut-side down, in a baking dish. Cover with aluminum foil and bake as directed.

Lumpia

Filipino-style egg rolls, or lumpia, are about 6 in/15 cm long and about as thick as a small cigar. Serve them as a delicious appetizer or first course.

INGREDIENTS

FILLING

2 oz/60 g chopped onion

2 cloves garlic, minced

1 teaspoon grated fresh ginger root

1 tablespoon cooking oil

4 oz/125 g finely chopped peeled and deveined shrimp (prawns)

4 oz/125 g finely chopped cooked pork

1/4 cup/2 fl oz/60 ml water

2 tablespoons soy sauce

1/8 teaspoon pepper

SAUCE

2 cloves garlic, minced

1 teaspoon cooking oil

1 teaspoon cornstarch (cornflour)

1/2 cup/4 fl oz/125 ml vinegar

2 tablespoons water

LUMPIA

12 lumpia wrappers (Filipino pastry wrappers) or spring roll wrappers

cooking oil, for frying

*Crisp lumpia are filled with
a mixture of shrimp and
pork, flavored with
spicy fresh ginger.
Serve as an hors
d'oeuvre or first
course with a
garlicky dipping sauce.*

Stuffed Pasta

Preparation Time 40 minutes
Cooking Time 6 to 9 minutes
Makes 12 rolls

For filling, in a large frying pan cook onion, garlic, and ginger root in hot oil for 5 minutes, or till tender, but not brown. Add shrimp and cook till they turn pink, stirring constantly. Add cooked pork, water, soy sauce, and pepper. Cook till liquid is evaporated.

Meanwhile, for sauce, in a small frying pan or saucepan cook garlic in hot oil till tender. In a small mixing bowl combine cornstarch, vinegar and water. Carefully add to pan. Cook and stir till sauce is slightly thickened and bubbly. Cook and stir for 1 minute more. Set aside.

To assemble lumpia, place a lumpia or spring roll wrapper on a flat surface in front of you. Spoon 2 tablespoons of the filling nearly across the width of the wrapper. Roll the wrapper once to cover the filling, then fold sides towards center. Moisten edges with water and continue to roll tightly.

In a large frying pan heat 1 in/2.5 cm of cooking oil to 365°F/185°C. Fry lumpia, a few at a time, for 2 to 3 minutes, or till golden. Drain on paper towels. Serve immediately with sauce.

Per serving 190 calories/798 kilojoules, 12 g protein, 14 g carbohydrate, 10 g total fat (2 g saturated), 68 mg cholesterol, 372 mg sodium, 186 mg potassium

STEP 1

Filling

Prepare the filling and place in a bowl nearby. Spoon 2 tablespoons of the filling across the width of each dough wrapper. Leave a slight margin of space at either end.

STEP 2

Rolling

Roll the wrapper once to cover the filling, then fold the sides toward the center. Moisten the edges with water and continue to roll tightly.

STEP 3

Frying

Heat oil to correct temperature in a large frying pan. Drop a few lumpia at a time into the hot oil with a wide metal spatula. Cook until golden brown, remove, and drain.

Ravioli with a filling of thyme-scented mushrooms: elegant fare for any special occasion.

Mushroom-filled Ravioli

A mixture of several types of mushrooms will add a deep, woody flavor to the ravioli filling. These make a beautiful first course, light supper, or hot hors d'oeuvre served in a chafing dish with toothpicks for spearing.

INGREDIENTS

2 portions (8 oz/250 g) spinach pasta (page 31)

FILLING

4 oz/125 g finely chopped fresh mushrooms

1 1/2 oz/45 g finely chopped onion

1 clove garlic, minced

1 tablespoon margarine or butter

1 beaten egg

1/4 cup/1 oz/30 g seasoned fine bread crumbs

1/4 cup/1 oz/30 g grated Parmesan cheese

1/4 teaspoon dried thyme, crushed

SAUCE

1/2 cup/8 fl oz/250 ml heavy (double) cream

fresh thyme leaves (optional)

Preparation Time 1 hour
Cooking Time 20 minutes
Serves 6 as a first course

METHOD FOR MAKING MUSHROOM-FILLED RAVIOLI

Prepare spinach pasta as directed, except roll each portion of dough into an 8x12-in/20x30-cm rectangle. Cover and set aside.

For filling, in a large frying pan cook mushrooms, onion, and garlic in hot margarine or butter for 5 minutes, or till tender. In a medium mixing bowl combine egg, bread crumbs, Parmesan cheese, and thyme. Stir in mushroom mixture. Set aside.

To make ravioli, cut each portion of pasta into four 2x12-in/5x30-cm strips. Brush one side of one strip with water. Place about 2 teaspoons of filling every 2 in/5 cm, beginning 1 in/2.5 cm from the end of one of the pieces. Take the second strip and place it over the top of the filling. Press pasta together between the mounds of filling. Use a 2-in/5-cm ravioli cutter, square biscuit cutter, or sharp knife to cut between the ravioli. Press the edges down firmly again to seal. Repeat with remaining pasta and filling.

For sauce, in a small saucepan heat cream over medium heat for about 15 minutes, or till bubbly, stirring frequently. Boil gently for 3 to 4 minutes more.

Meanwhile, in a large saucepan or pasta pot bring 12 cups/3 qt/ 3 l water to boiling. Add half the pasta. Reduce heat slightly. Boil, uncovered, for 6 to 8 minutes, or till al dente, stirring occasionally. Remove pasta from boiling water with a slotted spoon and place in a greased casserole. Cover and keep warm in a preheated 300°F/150°C/Gas Mark 2 oven while cooking remaining pasta. Pour thickened cream over cooked ravioli. If desired, sprinkle with fresh thyme. Serve immediately.

Per serving 262 calories/1,100 kilojoules, 7 g protein, 16 g carbohydrate, 20 g total fat (11 g saturated), 111 mg cholesterol, 301 mg sodium, 164 mg potassium

Meat-stuffed Ravioli

Using egg roll wrappers (wonton wrappers) will cut down on the preparation time
for this recipe. Substitute 48 wrappers for the pasta and cook for 6 to 8 minutes.

INGREDIENTS

2 portions (8 oz/250 g)
homemade pasta (page 28)

classic tomato sauce (page 41)
or 3 1/2 cups/28 fl oz/875 ml
canned or bottled Italian-style
tomato sauce

1 beaten egg

3/4 cup/1 1/2 oz/45 g soft bread
crumbs

2 tablespoons dry red wine

1 clove garlic, minced

1 teaspoon fennel seed, crushed

1/4 teaspoon Italian
seasoning, crushed

1/4 teaspoon salt

1/8 teaspoon pepper

12 oz/375 g lean ground
(minced) beef or veal

1/4 cup/1 oz/30 g grated
Parmesan cheese

Preparation Time 1 hour
Cooking Time 12 to 16 minutes
Serves 4 as a main course

Prepare fresh pasta as directed, except roll each portion of the dough into an 8x12-in/20x30-cm rectangle. Cover and set aside.

If using classic tomato sauce, prepare as directed. Set aside.

In a mixing bowl stir together egg, bread crumbs, wine, garlic, fennel seed, Italian seasoning, salt, and pepper. Add beef or veal and mix well. Shape meat mixture into a 6x4-in/15x10-cm rectangle. Cut into twenty-four 1-in/2.5-cm squares.

To make ravioli, cut each portion of pasta into four 2x12-in/5x30-cm strips. Brush one side of one strip with water. Place 1 meat square every 2 in/5 cm, beginning 1 in/2.5 cm from the end of one of the pieces. Take the second strip of pasta and place it over the top of the filling. Press pasta together between the meat squares. Use a 2-in/5-cm ravioli cutter, or sharp knife to cut between the ravioli. Press the edges down firmly again. Repeat with remaining pasta and filling.

Meanwhile, in a large saucepan or pasta pot bring 12 cups/3 qt/ 3 l water to boiling. Add half the ravioli. Reduce heat slightly. Boil, uncovered, for 6 to 8 minutes, or till meat in ravioli is no longer pink and pasta is al dente, stirring occasionally. Remove ravioli from boiling water with a slotted spoon and place in a greased casserole. Cover and keep warm in a preheated 300°F/150°C/Gas Mark 2 oven while cooking remaining ravioli. Serve tomato sauce over hot cooked ravioli. Sprinkle with Parmesan cheese and serve immediately.

Per serving 642 calories/2,696 kilojoules, 33 g protein, 77 g carbohydrate, 24 g total fat (6 g saturated), 165 mg cholesterol, 638 mg sodium, 1,576 mg potassium

With very little effort, you can make ravioli that compare to the best restaurant pasta. Serve with a simple tomato sauce, a salad, and garlic bread.

*Tiny stuffed tortellini are
made from little circles of
spinach pasta that are filled,
sealed, and folded in half.*

Ham Tortellini with Cheese Sauce

Here's an unusual pasta using a popular combination: ham and Swiss cheese.
Spinach pasta adds color and extra flavor to the dish.

INGREDIENTS

2 portions (8 oz/250 g) spinach
pasta (page 31)

FILLING

2 tablespoons finely chopped celery

2 tablespoons finely chopped onion

2 teaspoons margarine or butter

4 oz/125 g ground (minced)
cooked ham

1 beaten egg yolk

SAUCE

2 tablespoons margarine or butter

4 teaspoons all-purpose
(plain) flour

1 cup/8 fl oz/250 ml milk

1/2 cup/2 oz/60 g shredded
Swiss cheese

2 tablespoons chopped
fresh parsley

Preparation Time 1½ hours
Cooking Time 12 to 16 minutes
Serves 4 as a main course

METHOD FOR MAKING HAM TORTELLINI WITH CHEESE SAUCE

Per serving 317 calories/1,331 kilojoules,
17 g protein, 24 g carbohydrate,
17 g total fat (6 g saturated),
115 mg cholesterol, 592 mg sodium,
316 mg potassium

Prepare and roll spinach pasta as directed. With a 1½-in/4-cm round cutter, cut 96 circles from dough. Cover and set aside.

For filling, cook celery and onion in hot margarine or butter till tender. Remove from heat and stir in ham and egg yolk. Place about ¼ teaspoon of the filling in the center of each circle. Fold circle in half and press edges together. Place your finger against the fold and bring corners together, pressing to seal. Let stand for 10 minutes.

In a large saucepan or pasta pot bring 12 cups/3 qt/3 l water to boiling. Add half the tortellini. Reduce heat slightly. Boil, uncovered, for 6 to 8 minutes, or till al dente, stirring occasionally. Remove pasta from boiling water with a slotted spoon and place in a greased casserole. Cover and keep warm in a preheated 300°F/150°C/Gas Mark 2 oven while cooking remaining pasta.

Meanwhile, for sauce, in a small saucepan melt margarine or butter. Stir in flour. Add milk all at once. Cook and stir till thickened and bubbly. Cook and stir for 1 minute more. Stir in Swiss cheese and parsley till cheese is melted.

Spoon sauce over hot cooked tortellini and serve immediately.

Agnolotti Florentine with Mornay Sauce

Agnolotti ("fat little lambs") and ravioli are essentially the same dish, except that the former are shaped into half-moons while ravioli are square. Tomato or spinach pasta (page 31) complements the spinach filling and the creamy cheese sauce.

INGREDIENTS

SPINACH AGNOLOTTI

4 portions (1 lb/500 g) tomato or spinach pasta (page 31)

5 oz/155 g fresh spinach or frozen chopped spinach, cooked and well drained

1 egg yolk

1/3 cup/3 oz/90 g packaged cream cheese with chives, softened

1 oz/30 g finely chopped prosciutto

2 tablespoons grated Parmesan cheese

1/8 teaspoon ground nutmeg

MORNAY SAUCE

2 tablespoons margarine or butter

2 tablespoons all-purpose (plain) flour

1 1/4 cups/10 fl oz/315 ml milk

1 cup/4 oz/125 g shredded fontina or Jarlsberg cheese

METHOD FOR MAKING AGNOLOTTI FLORENTINE WITH MORNAY SAUCE

Preparation Time 1½ hours
Cooking Time 16 to 20 minutes
Serves 6 as an accompaniment or
first course

STEPS AT A GLANCE	Page
▦ Making pasta	**12–31**
▦ Grating nutmeg	**47**
▦ Stuffing pasta	**230–235**

For spinach agnolotti, prepare fresh pasta as directed, except roll each portion of the dough into an 8x12-in/20x30-cm rectangle. Cover and set aside. In a food processor bowl or blender container process or blend cooked spinach and 1 egg yolk till nearly smooth. Transfer mixture to a medium mixing bowl and stir in cream cheese, prosciutto, Parmesan cheese, and nutmeg. Cover and refrigerate till needed.

Cut dough into circles with a 2-in/5-cm fluted cutter, place about ½ teaspoon of filling on each round, brush edge with water, then fold in half to create a half-moon shape. Repeat with remaining pasta and filling.

For mornay sauce, in a small saucepan melt margarine or butter. Stir in flour. Add milk all at once. Cook and stir over medium heat till thickened and bubbly. Cook and stir for 1 minute more. Stir in fontina or Jarlsberg cheese till melted. Cover sauce and keep warm.

Meanwhile, in a large saucepan or pasta pot bring 12 cups/3 qt/ 3 l water to boiling. Add half the pasta. Reduce heat slightly. Boil, uncovered, for 8 to 10 minutes, or till al dente, stirring occasionally. Remove pasta from boiling water with a slotted spoon and place in a greased casserole. Cover and keep warm in a preheated 300°F/150°C/Gas Mark 2 oven while cooking remaining pasta. Spoon mornay sauce over hot cooked pasta and serve immediately.

Per serving 304 calories/1,277 kilojoules, 15 g protein, 18 g carbohydrate, 19 g total fat (7 g saturated), 140 mg cholesterol, 283 mg sodium, 199 mg potassium

Pasta dough may be cut into rounds with a plain or scalloped cutter. They are filled with spinach, ham, and cheeses, then folded into charming half-moons.

Sausage and peppers, a very compatible duo, stand out in a highly seasoned tomato sauce for cheese tortellini.

Cheese Tortellini with Sausage & Peppers

This deep-red spicy sauce isn't shy. It is assertively seasoned with crushed red pepper, garlic, and wine, a nice contrast to the mildness of the cheese-filled tortellini.

INGREDIENTS

12 oz/375 g Italian-style sausages

1 cup/8 fl oz/250 ml water

4 oz/125 g chopped onion

2 cloves garlic, minced

2 teaspoons olive oil or cooking oil

28 oz/875 g canned Italian-style tomatoes, cut up, with juice

1/4 cup/2 fl oz/60 ml tomato paste

1/4 cup/2 fl oz/60 ml dry red wine

2 tablespoons chopped fresh parsley

1 teaspoon dried oregano, crushed

1/4 teaspoon crushed red pepper (chili) flakes

1 medium green pepper (capsicum), cut into 1/2 in/12 mm pieces

12 oz/375 g dried or 1 lb/500 g fresh cheese-filled tortellini or ravioli, or spinach agnolotti (page 259)

263

Preparation Time 45 minutes
Cooking Time 20 minutes
Serves 4 to 5 as a main course

In a large frying pan combine sausages and water. Bring to boiling; reduce heat. Cover and simmer for 15 minutes, or till juices run clear. Drain off water. Cook sausages, uncovered, for 2 to 4 minutes more, or till brown, turning frequently. Remove from pan; cool. Bias-slice into 1/2-in/12-mm pieces. Wipe pan clean with paper towels.

In the same pan, cook onion and garlic in hot oil till tender but not brown. Stir in tomatoes, tomato paste, wine, parsley, oregano, and crushed red pepper flakes. Add sausage and green pepper to pan. Bring to boiling; reduce heat. Cover and simmer for 20 minutes, or to desired consistency.

Meanwhile, in a large saucepan or pasta pot bring 16 cups/4 qt/4 l water to boiling. Add pasta. Reduce heat slightly. Boil, uncovered, 15 minutes for dried pasta or 8 to 10 minutes for fresh, or till al dente, stirring occasionally. (Or, cook according to package directions.) Drain immediately. Return pasta to warm saucepan. Pour sausage mixture over hot cooked pasta. Serve immediately.

Per serving 654 calories/2,747 kilojoules, 35 g protein, 73 g carbohydrate, 24 g total fat (6 g saturated), 111 mg cholesterol, 1,441 mg sodium, 946 mg potassium

Ravioli with Walnut Sauce

Using bought fresh ravioli makes this a quick and easy meal to whip up after a busy day. If you prefer, serve the sauce over your own homemade ravioli (pages 250 and 253).

INGREDIENTS

9 oz/280 g purchased fresh ravioli or homemade mushroom-filled ravioli (page 250) or meat-stuffed ravioli (page 253)

¼ cup/1 oz/30 g chopped walnuts, pecans, or almonds

4 scallions (spring onions), thinly sliced

1 teaspoon grated ginger root

3 tablespoons margarine or butter

¼ cup/1½ oz/45 g crumbled blue cheese, feta cheese, or grated Parmesan cheese (optional)

Preparation Time 15 minutes
Cooking Time 3 to 4 minutes
Serves 4 as a main course

METHOD FOR MAKING RAVIOLI WITH WALNUT SAUCE

In a large saucepan or pasta pot bring 12 cups/3 qt/3 l water to boiling. Add pasta. Reduce heat slightly. Boil, uncovered, for 6 to 8 minutes, or till al dente, stirring occasionally. (Or, cook according to package directions.) Drain immediately.

Meanwhile, in a medium frying pan cook and stir the nuts, scallions, and ginger in hot margarine or butter for 3 to 4 minutes, or till scallions are tender but not brown and nuts are lightly toasted. Pour nut mixture over hot cooked ravioli. If desired, sprinkle with blue cheese, feta cheese, or Parmesan cheese. Serve immediately.

Per serving 360 calories/1,512 kilojoules, 13 g protein, 21 g carbohydrate, 25 g total fat (4 g saturated), 59 mg cholesterol, 538 mg sodium, 79 mg potassium

Grated fresh ginger, quickly sautéed with chopped scallion and walnuts, adds a refreshing note to an easy pasta dish. Top with tangy crumbled blue cheese or feta cheese.

Green, red and yellow peppers, squash, zucchini, and tomatoes add the bright colors and sun-drenched flavors of an Italian kitchen garden to cheese-filled manicotti.

Manicotti with Roasted Vegetables

To make fresh manicotti shells, use two portions of homemade pasta (page 28).
Roll dough into a 14x10-in/35x25-cm rectangle about ⅛ in/3 mm thick.
Cut the dough into eight 5x3½-in/13x9-cm rectangles. Cook for
2 to 3 minutes and continue as directed, following the directions
for filling manicotti on page 240.

INGREDIENTS

½ a medium green pepper
(capsicum)

½ a medium orange or red
pepper (capsicum)

½ a medium yellow pepper
(capsicum)

½ a medium onion

1 medium yellow squash

1 medium zucchini (courgette)

2 cloves garlic, peeled

1 tablespoon olive oil or
cooking oil

classic tomato sauce (page 41)
or 3½ cups/28 fl oz/875 ml
canned or bottled Italian-style
tomato sauce

8 dried manicotti shells

2 beaten eggs

2 cups/8oz/250 g shredded
mozzarella cheese

1½ cups/12 oz/375 g ricotta
cheese

⅓ cup/1½ oz/45 g grated
Parmesan cheese

2 tablespoons chopped fresh
chives

¼ teaspoon ground white
or black pepper

METHOD FOR MAKING MANICOTTI WITH ROASTED VEGETABLES

Preparation Time 1 hour
(includes sauce)
Baking Time 65 to 75 minutes
Serves 4 to 6 as a main course

STEPS AT A GLANCE	Page
Classic tomato sauce	**41**
Cooking pasta	**22–27**
Chopping chives	**81**
Stuffing manicotti & cannelloni	**236–241**

Cut the peppers into bite-size strips. Cut the onion into small wedges. Bias-slice the squash and zucchini into ¼-in/6-mm-thick pieces. In a 13x9x2-in/33x23x5-cm baking dish combine the peppers, onion, squash and zucchini, and garlic. Drizzle with olive oil or cooking oil. Bake in a preheated 425°F/210°C/Gas Mark 5 oven for about 30 minutes, or till

tender, stirring once or twice. Remove garlic cloves. Reduce oven temperature to 350°F/180°C/Gas Mark 4.

Meanwhile, if using classic tomato sauce, prepare as directed. Set aside. In a large saucepan or pasta pot bring 12 cups/3 qt/3 l water to boiling. Add manicotti shells. Reduce heat slightly. Boil, uncovered, about 18 minutes, or till al dente, stirring occasionally. (Or, cook according to package directions.) Remove and drain immediately. Rinse with cold water and drain again.

In a medium mixing bowl stir together the eggs, mozzarella cheese, ricotta cheese, Parmesan cheese, chives, and pepper. To fill manicotti shells, spoon equal portions of the cheese mixture into each one. Arrange manicotti in a 12-cup/3-qt/3-1 rectangular baking dish. Pour tomato sauce over the top. Arrange roasted vegetables on top of the sauce. Bake, covered, in the 350°F/180°C/Gas Mark 4 oven for 35 to 40 minutes, or till heated through.

Roll cooked pasta squares or rectangles around the filling of your choice, top with a simple tomato sauce and bake.

Per serving 720 calories/3,024 kilojoules, 41 g protein, 67 g carbohydrate, 34 g total fat (14 g saturated), 174 mg cholesterol, 885 mg sodium, 1,726 mg potassium

Broiled Spinach Cannelloni

To save time, use 6 dried lasagne noodles instead of making the fresh pasta. Cook the noodles according to package directions and drain. Cut each noodle into 3 pieces for 9 servings. Spoon the filling onto the pasta and continue as directed in the recipe.

INGREDIENTS

CANNELLONI

1 portion (4 oz/125 g) homemade pasta (page 28)

5 oz/155 g fresh spinach or frozen chopped spinach, thawed

3 or 4 cloves garlic, peeled and quartered

2 tablespoons olive oil or cooking oil

1/4 cup/1 oz/30 g grated Parmesan cheese

2 tablespoons fine dry bread crumbs

2 teaspoons olive oil or cooking oil

1/8 teaspoon ground red pepper (cayenne)

1 tablespoon grated Parmesan cheese

SAUCE

1/2 cup/4 fl oz/125 ml chicken stock

1 1/2 teaspoons cornstarch (cornflour)

1 teaspoon margarine or butter

1 tablespoon lemon juice

1 tablespoon heavy (double) cream

1/4 cup/1 1/2 oz/45 g toasted pine nuts

Preparation Time 1 hour
Broiling Time 5 minutes
Serves 8 as an accompaniment or first course

Spinach-filled pasta tubes are placed under the grill for a golden-brown finish, then served with a lemony cream sauce and pine nuts.

METHOD FOR MAKING BROILED SPINACH CANNELLONI

For cannelloni, prepare and roll homemade pasta as directed. Cut into sixteen 3-in/7.5-cm squares. Cover and set aside.

Trim and wash fresh spinach, if using; finely chop. In a large frying pan cook and stir garlic in 2 tablespoons hot olive oil or cooking oil over medium-high heat for 30 seconds. Add fresh or thawed frozen spinach. Cook and stir for 1 to 2 minutes, or till fresh spinach is wilted or thawed spinach is heated through. Drain thoroughly in a colander, cool, and squeeze out excess liquid. In a medium mixing bowl combine spinach, 1/4 cup/1 oz/30 g Parmesan cheese, bread crumbs, and the ground red pepper.

Meanwhile, in a large saucepan or pasta pot bring 12 cups/3 qt/ 3 l water to boiling. Add pasta. Reduce heat slightly. Boil, stirring occasionally, uncovered, for 3 to 4 minutes, or till al dente. Use a slotted spoon to carefully lift pasta out of water and into a colander. Rinse with cold water. Drain well. Carefully spread on a damp cloth towel.

To assemble, place 1 scant tablespoon filling along one end of each pasta square. Roll the dough tightly around the filling. Place on a greased baking sheet. Drizzle 2 teaspoons olive oil over pasta. Sprinkle with 1 tablespoon Parmesan cheese. Broil 6 in/15 cm from the heat for 5 minutes, or till golden.

Meanwhile, for sauce, in a small saucepan combine chicken stock and cornstarch; add margarine or butter. Cook and stir till thickened and bubbly. Stir in lemon juice and cream and heat through. Spoon over cannelloni; sprinkle with toasted pine nuts.

Per serving 182 calories/764 kilojoules, 7 g protein, 20 g carbohydrate, 10 g total fat (2 g saturated), 10 mg cholesterol, 147 mg sodium, 261 mg potassium

Classic Cannelloni

Both the tomato sauce and chicken filling can be prepared a day ahead and refrigerated until you assemble the cannelloni. Let the sauce and filling sit at room temperature for about 15 minutes so they will bake in the specified time.

INGREDIENTS

1 portion (4 oz/125 g) homemade pasta (page 28)

1 1/2 cups/12 fl oz/375 ml classic tomato sauce (page 41) or canned or bottled Italian-style tomato sauce

PARMESAN SAUCE

2 oz/60 g margarine or butter

1/4 cup/1 oz/30 g all-purpose (plain) flour

1/4 teaspoon salt

1/8 teaspoon pepper

1 1/2 cups/12 fl oz/375 ml milk

3/4 cup/1 1/2 oz/45 g grated Parmesan cheese

1/4 cup/2 fl oz/60 ml sour cream

CHICKEN FILLING

1 tablespoon olive oil or cooking oil

8 oz/250 g boneless, skinless chicken breast halves (fillets), chopped

2 oz/60 g chopped onion

1 oz/30 g chopped fresh parsley

1 clove garlic, minced

2 oz/60 g sliced prosciutto or ham, chopped

1 tablespoon grated Parmesan cheese

Preparation Time 1 1/2 hours
Baking Time 30 to 35 minutes
Serves 4 as a main course or 8 as a first course

275

Two sauces, one made with fresh tomatoes and the other a béchamel, top homemade cannelloni.

METHOD FOR MAKING CLASSIC CANNELLONI

Roll out homemade pasta as directed. Cut into sixteen 3-in/7.5-cm squares. Cover and set aside. Prepare classic tomato sauce as directed, set aside.

For Parmesan sauce, in a small saucepan melt margarine or butter. Stir in flour, salt, and pepper. Add milk all at once. Cook and stir over medium heat till thickened and bubbly. Stir in Parmesan cheese and sour cream. Set aside.

For chicken filling, heat oil in a large frying pan. Add chicken, onion, parsley, garlic, and salt and pepper to taste. Cook for 5 minutes, or till chicken is tender and no longer pink. Cool slightly. Process chicken mixture and prosciutto or ham in a food processor bowl or blender container till mixture is finely chopped. Do not over-process. Transfer the filling to a medium mixing bowl and add ¾ cup/ 6 fl oz/185 ml of the Parmesan sauce. Stir in well.

In a large saucepan or pasta pot bring 12 cups/3 qt/3 l water to boiling. Add pasta. Reduce heat slightly. Uncover pan and boil for 3 to 4 minutes, or till al dente. Drain.

Place a scant 2 tablespoons of the chicken filling along one edge of each pasta square. Roll dough tightly around the filling. Place in a greased 12-cup/3-qt/ 3-l rectangular baking dish. Pour remaining Parmesan sauce over half the pasta. Pour tomato sauce over remaining pasta. Sprinkle with 1 tablespoon Parmesan cheese. Bake in a preheated 350°F/180°C/Gas Mark 4 oven for 30 to 35 minutes, or till heated through. Serve immediately.

Per serving 490 calories/2,058 kilojoules, 27 g protein, 35 g carbohydrate, 28 g total fat (10 g saturated), 81 mg cholesterol, 1,066 mg sodium, 964 mg potassium

Stuffed Pasta

PASTA SALADS

BASIC TOOLS FOR MAKING PASTA SALADS

Always drain pasta thoroughly in a colander or strainer before tossing with other ingredients in a wide, shallow bowl. A small glass jar with a lid is handy for blending and storing salad dressings.

serving bowl

colander

screw-top jar

serving fork and spoon

Making Pasta Salads

Not surprisingly, pasta has the same affinity with salad dressings as it does with other sauces. Bathed in herb-flavored emulsions of fruity olive oil and tart vinegar, or tossed with creamy yogurt or sour cream blends, pasta absorbs some of the dressing and releases wonderful flavor with each bite. Shaped pasta, such as radiatori or conchiglie are especially good in salads. The tender chewiness of pasta contributes substance and textural contrast to a salad and holds its own against other additions like ripe olives, crunchy bits of celery and pepper, chunks of spicy salami, and toasted chopped nuts.

Pasta salads are delicious warm-weather companions to grilled meats, poultry, and fish. As main courses, they make appealing light lunches or suppers when accompanied with sliced fruit and a good, crusty loaf. They are simple to put together and can be assembled just far enough in advance to marry the flavors.

Pasta for salad should always be cooked just until al dente, never a second more. Nothing is worse than pasta that is too soft or that falls apart when the salad is tossed together. Drain the pasta thoroughly as soon as it is done, then rinse to stop the cooking and prevent the pasta from sticking together. Give it a good shake in the colander to pull off any water that remains. If water clings to the pasta, the flavor of the dressing will be diluted, much as it is when mixed with salad greens that haven't been dried properly.

If the dressing calls for olive oil, use a good one. The best are extra-virgin oils, from the first pressing of the olive. These oils vary in their fruitiness and offer a spectrum of color that ranges from verdant green to a golden bronze. Purchase small amounts of several different kinds until you find one or two that please you. Experiment with vinegars as well. A wide variety is available to give your dressings excitement, from deep-toned, sweet and mellow balsamic (the best comes from Modena in Italy), to red and white wine vinegars with delicate infusions of herbs or fruit.

Although this salad (page 304) specifies crinkled radiatori ("radiators"), you can substitute conchiglie ("shells") or any pasta of the same approximate size.

drain away as much water as possible after rinsing so none remains to dilute the dressing

STEP 1

Rinsing Pasta

Cook the pasta in 12 cups/3 qt/3 l of rapidly boiling water until it is al dente. Immediately drain off the cooking water. Rinse under cold running water to separate the pasta; drain again thoroughly

dressings with a mayonnaise base blend better when whisked in a bowl

STEP 2

Making Salad Dressing

Place all ingredients in a glass jar with a lid. Secure the lid and shake vigorously until the ingredients are combined into an emulsion.

mix thoroughly, but with a light touch

STEP 3

Tossing Salad

Place all the salad ingredients in a wide, shallow serving bowl. Pour the dressing over the pasta mixture. With a large spoon and fork or two spoons, toss gently to coat all the ingredients with dressing.

Pasta salads don't have to be served in a bowl: a thick slice of toasted focaccia piled with a simple pasta salad makes a great lunch. Here, shell pasta is mixed with cherry tomatoes, black olives, crumbled goat cheese and toasted pine nuts, then tossed in a basil vinaigrette.

Serve any grilled chicken or fish with this pasta salad that features the flavors of an Indian curry.

Curried Orzo Salad

Here we've used orzo, a barley-shaped pasta, in place of rice for a colorful
and refreshing salad with an Indian flavor. Other tiny pasta,
such as rosamarina or riso, can also be used.

INGREDIENTS

6 oz/185 g orzo pasta

3/4 cup/5 oz/155 g chopped
prosciutto or cooked ham

2 oranges, peeled, sectioned, and
cut into bite-size pieces

5 oz/155 g chopped celery

2 oz/60 g chopped green pepper
(capsicum)

4 scallions (spring onions),
thinly sliced

1/3 cup/2 1/2 oz/75 g mayonnaise
or salad dressing

1/3 cup/2 1/2 oz/75 g plain yogurt

2 tablespoons chutney, chopped

3/4 teaspoon curry powder

1 to 2 tablespoons milk
(optional)

1/3 cup/2 oz/60 g peanuts

Preparation Time 25 minutes
Cooking Time 5 to 8 minutes
Chilling Time 2 to 24 hours
Serves 6 as an accompaniment
or first course

METHOD FOR MAKING CURRIED ORZO SALAD

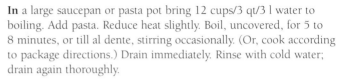

In a large saucepan or pasta pot bring 12 cups/3 qt/3 l water to boiling. Add pasta. Reduce heat slightly. Boil, uncovered, for 5 to 8 minutes, or till al dente, stirring occasionally. (Or, cook according to package directions.) Drain immediately. Rinse with cold water; drain again thoroughly.

In a large bowl combine cooked pasta, prosciutto or ham, oranges, celery, pepper, and scallions.

In a small mixing bowl stir together mayonnaise or salad dressing, yogurt, chutney, and curry powder. Stir into pasta mixture. Cover and refrigerate for 2 to 24 hours.

Just before serving, if necessary, stir in milk to moisten salad. Sprinkle with peanuts before serving.

Per serving 328 calories/1,377 kilojoules, 11 g protein, 33 g carbohydrate, 18 g total fat (2 g saturated), 8 mg cholesterol, 384 mg sodium, 236 mg potassium

STEP 1

Cutting the Peel from an Orange

Slice off the top and bottom of an orange with a sharp paring knife. Set one flat end on a cutting board. Hold the orange and, working from top to bottom, cut off 1-in/2.5-cm-wide strips of peel.

STEP 2

Sectioning an Orange

Work over a bowl to catch the juice. Insert a paring knife between the flesh and membrane of one section. Cut down to the center of the fruit. Turn the knife and slide it up the other side of the section to release it from the membrane on that side. Repeat with remaining sections.

Eggplant Salad Shells

Make this earthy eggplant filling the night before so that all the flavors have a chance to mix. Serve as an hors d'oeuvre, or as part of a cold buffet.

INGREDIENTS

1 medium eggplant (aubergine), peeled and cut into 1/2 in/12 mm cubes

1 1/2 oz/45 g chopped onion

1 1/2 oz/45 g chopped celery

1/4 cup/2 fl oz/60 ml olive oil or cooking oil

14 oz/440 g canned diced peeled tomatoes, with juice

3 tablespoons red wine vinegar

2 tablespoons tomato paste

1 teaspoon sugar

1/2 teaspoon salt

dash ground red pepper (cayenne)

1 tablespoon chopped fresh parsley

1 tablespoon capers, drained

2 1/2 oz/75 g black or kalamata olives, pitted and sliced

2 tablespoons toasted pine nuts or chopped almonds

18 conchiglioni (large pasta shells), about 4 oz/125 g

Big pasta shells filled with fresh vegetables are easily eaten with the fingers. They are ideal buffet fare.

METHOD FOR MAKING EGGPLANT SALAD SHELLS

Preparation Time 1¼ hours
Chilling Time 2 to 24 hours
Cooking Time 23 to 25 minutes
Makes 18 shells

In a large frying pan cook eggplant, onion, and celery in hot oil, covered, over medium heat for 5 to 8 minutes, or just till tender, stirring occasionally. Stir in the undrained tomatoes, wine vinegar, tomato paste, sugar, salt, and red pepper. Cook, uncovered, over low heat for 5 minutes, or to desired consistency, stirring occasionally. Remove from heat. Stir in parsley and capers. Cool. Cover and refrigerate for 2 to 24 hours.

Let the eggplant mixture stand at room temperature for 30 minutes. Stir in olives and pine nuts.

Meanwhile, in a large saucepan or pasta pot bring 12 cups/3 qt/3 l water to boiling. Add pasta shells. Reduce heat slightly. Boil, uncovered, for 23 to 25 minutes, or till al dente, stirring occasionally. (Or, follow package directions.) Drain. Rinse with cold water; drain again thoroughly. Pat dry with paper towels.

To assemble, fill each shell with equal amounts of the eggplant mixture. Serve immediately.

Per serving 235 calories/987 kilojoules, 5 g protein, 28 g carbohydrate, 13 g total fat (2 g saturated), 0 mg cholesterol, 381 mg sodium, 472 mg potassium

STEP 1

Stuffing Shells

Cup a cooked pasta shell in one hand and squeeze at both ends to open it. Scoop up some of the filling with a small spoon and insert in the shell. Repeat with the remaining shells and filling.

A mixed salad is always more interesting when the shapes, colors, and textures vary. Here rotini attractively contrast with other ingredients cut into cubes, thin strips, and half-rounds.

Hero Pasta Salad

This salad lends itself well to improvisation. Try adding some sliced kalamata olives, capers, chopped peppers, or yellow or orange tomatoes. If making it ahead, wait to add the lettuce and tomato until just before serving time.

INGREDIENTS

SALAD

3 oz/90 g rotini, cavatelli, or other dried shaped pasta

4 oz/125 g cubed provolone cheese

2 oz/60 g cooked ham, cut into thin bite-size strips

2 oz/60 g hard salami, chopped

1 small red onion, halved then sliced

4 oz/125 g pepperoncini, sliced, or sliced bell pepper (capsicum) rings

6 oz/185 g shredded iceberg or romaine (cos) lettuce

1 large tomato, coarsely chopped, or 4 oz/125 g cherry tomatoes, halved

DRESSING

3 tablespoons olive oil or salad oil

3 tablespoons balsamic vinegar

1 tablespoon chopped fresh oregano or 1/2 teaspoon dried oregano, crushed

2 small cloves garlic, minced

1/4 teaspoon dry mustard

1/8 teaspoon coarsely ground black pepper

Preparation Time 20 minutes
Cooking Time 8 to 12 minutes
Serves 4 as a main course

In a large saucepan or pasta pot bring 12 cups/3 qt/3 l water to boiling. Add pasta. Reduce heat slightly. Boil, uncovered, for 8 to 12 minutes, or till pasta is al dente, stirring occasionally. (Or, cook according to package directions.) Drain immediately. Rinse with cold water and drain again thoroughly.

In a large bowl toss together cooked pasta, provolone cheese, ham, salami, onion, and pepperoncini or pepper rings. Add lettuce and tomato; gently toss to mix.

In a screw-top jar combine olive oil or salad oil, vinegar, oregano, garlic, dry mustard, and pepper. Cover; shake well. Pour over pasta mixture; toss to coat all ingredients with dressing and serve.

Per serving 426 calories/1,789 kilojoules, 20 g protein, 30 g carbohydrate, 25 g total fat (9 g saturated), 39 mg cholesterol, 1,080 mg sodium, 449 mg potassium

STEPS FOR SHREDDING LETTUCE AND SLICING ONION

STEP 1

Shredding Lettuce

Hold one quarter of a head of iceberg lettuce firmly against a cutting board. Using a sharp knife, slice the lettuce thinly. The slices will separate into long, thin shreds. Wash and drain if necessary.

STEP 2

Slicing Onion

Peel the onion and cut in half lengthwise from top to root end. Place on a cutting board, cut-side down. Hold firmly and cut crosswise into 1/8-in/3-mm-thick slices. The slices will separate into half circles and then into small pieces.

Broiled Tuna & White Bean Salad

If you have any leftover salad, refrigerate it, but be sure to bring it back to room temperature before serving it again, or the dressing will be thick and lumpy.

INGREDIENTS

12 oz/375 g fresh or frozen tuna steaks, 1/2 in/12 mm thick, or 12 oz/375 g canned white tuna, drained and broken into chunks

olive oil or salad oil

8 oz/250 g penne or other dried shaped pasta

20 oz/625 g canned cannellini or white kidney beans, drained and rinsed

2 medium tomatoes, coarsely chopped

1/2 a medium yellow pepper (capsicum), cut into thin bite-size strips

1/2 cup/4 fl oz/125 ml olive oil or salad oil

1/4 cup/2 fl oz/60 ml lemon juice

2 shallots, finely chopped

2 tablespoons chopped fresh basil or 1 teaspoon dried basil, crushed

1/4 teaspoon salt

1/8 teaspoon pepper

This is no ordinary tuna salad. It combines fresh tuna with cannellini beans, tomatoes, yellow pepper, and penne pasta, all bathed in a lemon-and-herb dressing.

Preparation Time 30 minutes
Broiling Time 4 to 6 minutes
Cooking Time 12 to 14 minutes
Serves 4 to 6 as a main course

STEPS AT A GLANCE   Page

If using tuna steaks, thaw if frozen. Measure thickness of fish. Brush each side of tuna with oil. Broil tuna for 4 to 6 minutes per ½-in/12-mm thickness, or till tuna flakes easily when tested with a fork, turning once. Slice tuna diagonally into thin strips.

In a large saucepan or pasta pot bring 12 cups/3 qt/3 l water to boiling. Add pasta. Reduce heat slightly. Boil, uncovered, for 12 to 14 minutes, or till al dente, stirring occasionally. (Or, cook according to package directions.) Drain immediately.

In a large bowl combine cooked fresh or canned tuna, hot cooked pasta, beans, tomatoes, and yellow pepper.

For dressing, in a screw-top jar combine ½ cup/4 fl oz/125 ml olive oil or salad oil, lemon juice, shallots, basil, salt, and pepper. Pour dressing over pasta; toss gently and serve.

Per serving 519 calories/2,180 kilojoules, 16 g protein, 59 g carbohydrate, 28 g total fat (4 g saturated), 1 mg cholesterol, 369 mg sodium, 493 mg potassium

Warm Tomato-Feta Cheese Salad

Pasta goes Greek. For a stronger and more authentic Greek flavor, use kalamata olives rather than pitted black olives. If you refrigerate any leftover salad, bring it to room temperature before serving.

INGREDIENTS

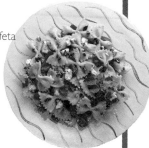

3 ripe tomatoes or 6 ripe plum (Roma) tomatoes, seeded and chopped

3 tablespoons olive oil or salad oil

3 tablespoons lemon juice

1/2 oz/15 g chopped fresh oregano or 1 teaspoon dried oregano, crushed

2 cloves garlic, minced

1/8 teaspoon pepper

2 cups/8 oz/250 g crumbled feta cheese

2oz/60 g kalamata olives, pitted and chopped, or pitted black olives, chopped

8 oz/250 g dried farfalle or conchiglie, or 1 lb/500 g fresh farfalle

Preparation Time 50 minutes
Cooking Time 10 to 12 minutes
Serves 8 to 10 as an accompaniment or first course

Warm pasta tossed with marinated tomatoes, olives, and cheese makes a salad that's full of flavor.

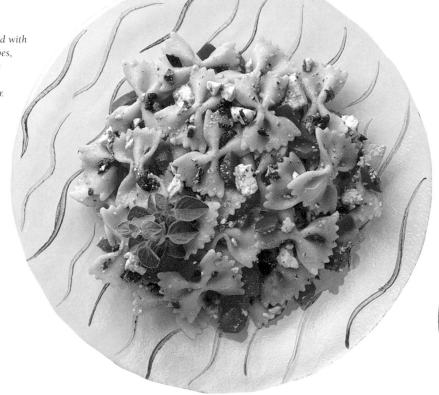

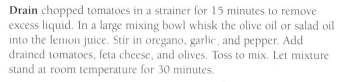

Drain chopped tomatoes in a strainer for 15 minutes to remove excess liquid. In a large mixing bowl whisk the olive oil or salad oil into the lemon juice. Stir in oregano, garlic, and pepper. Add drained tomatoes, feta cheese, and olives. Toss to mix. Let mixture stand at room temperature for 30 minutes.

Meanwhile, in a large saucepan or pasta pot bring 12 cups/3 qt/3 l water to boiling. Add pasta. Reduce heat slightly. Boil, uncovered, for 10 to 12 minutes for dried pasta or 2 to 3 minutes for fresh, or till al dente, stirring occasionally. (Or, cook according to package directions.) Drain immediately. Return pasta to warm saucepan. Add tomato mixture to hot cooked pasta and toss well, to combine all ingredients. Serve immediately.

Per serving 346 calories/1,453 kilojoules, 14 g protein, 29 g carbohydrate, 20 g total fat (10 g saturated), 57 mg cholesterol, 741 mg sodium, 187 mg potassium

Pasta Salad with Walnut Dressing

Volunteer to bring this easy salad when you're asked to a casual gathering.
Combine the ingredients at home, but don't add the dressing
until you get to the party.

INGREDIENTS

8 oz/250 g tricolored or plain radiatori

1 cup/4 oz/125 g chopped toasted walnuts

4 oz/125 g capicollo or cooked ham, cut into small cubes

1 cup/4 oz/125 g crumbled basil-and-tomato feta cheese or plain feta cheese

2¹/₂ oz/75 g pitted or unstuffed green olives

¹/₄ cup/2 fl oz/60 ml olive oil or salad oil

¹/₄ cup/2 fl oz/60 ml fresh lime juice

¹/₂ oz/15 g chopped fresh parsley

1 clove garlic, minced

¹/₄ teaspoon salt

¹/₈ teaspoon pepper

red-tipped (oak) leaf lettuce

Preparation Time 30 minutes
Cooking Time 10 to 12 minutes
Serves 4 as a main course

A dressing tangy with lime coats chunks of ham and cheese, olives, toasted walnuts, and multicolored pasta.

In a large saucepan or pasta pot bring 12 cups/3 qt/3 l water to boiling. Add pasta. Reduce heat slightly. Boil, uncovered, for 10 to 12 minutes, or till al dente, stirring occasionally. (Or, cook according to package directions.) Drain immediately. Rinse with cold water; drain again thoroughly.

In a large bowl combine pasta, walnuts, capicollo or ham, feta cheese, and olives.

In a screw-top jar combine oil, lime juice, parsley, garlic, salt, and pepper. Cover and shake well. Pour over pasta mixture and gently toss to coat all ingredients with dressing.

Serve salad on lettuce leaves.

Per serving 691 calories/2,902 kilojoules, 24 g protein, 55 g carbohydrate, 44 g total fat (9 g saturated), 42 mg cholesterol, 922 mg sodium, 425 mg potassium

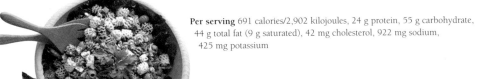

Tortellini-Mozzarella Salad

If you need to make the salad ahead of time, reserve the mozzarella and add it right before serving time so it doesn't become mushy or rubbery.

INGREDIENTS

5 oz/155 g dried or
10 oz/315 g fresh meat-filled
tortellini

1 1/2 cups/6 oz/185 g cubed plain
or smoked mozzarella

1/2 a medium red or yellow
pepper (capsicum), cubed

1/2 oz/15 g chopped fresh basil
or 1 teaspoon dried basil,
crushed

3 tablespoons olive oil
or salad oil

2 tablespoons
white wine vinegar

1 tablespoon
balsamic vinegar

1 small head
radicchio, divided
into leaf cups,
or 4 large lettuce leaves

Little leaves of radicchio serve as edible bowls for individual portions of tortellini salad.

METHOD FOR MAKING TORTELLINI-MOZZARELLA SALAD

Preparation Time 20 minutes
Cooking Time 15 minutes
Serves 4 as a main course

In a large saucepan or pasta pot bring 12 cups/3 qt/3 l water to boiling. Add pasta. Reduce heat slightly. Boil, uncovered, 15 minutes for dried pasta and 8 to 10 minutes for fresh, or till al dente, stirring occasionally. (Or, cook according to package directions.) Drain immediately. Rinse with cold water; drain again thoroughly.

In a medium mixing bowl combine cooked tortellini, mozzarella cheese, and red or yellow pepper.

In a screw-top jar combine basil, oil, white wine vinegar, and balsamic vinegar. Cover; shake well. Pour over pasta mixture and gently toss to coat all ingredients with dressing. Serve salad in radicchio cups or on lettuce leaves.

Per serving 320 calories/1,344 kilojoules, 15 g protein, 21 g carbohydrate, 19 g total fat (8 g saturated), 46 mg cholesterol, 381 mg sodium, 206 mg potassium

Glossary

Here you'll find information on selecting, purchasing, and storing ingredients used in this book

ARTICHOKES

Only the fleshy base of the leaves and the meaty bottom of this edible bud of a tall, thistle-like plant are eaten; the rest of the leaf and the fuzzy interior choke are discarded. Artichokes are sold fresh in sizes ranging from very small to very large; they are also available frozen, canned, and marinated. Select compact, heavy globes with tightly closed leaves; refrigerate in a plastic bag for up to 4 days.

ASPARAGUS

This tender stalk with a tightly closed bud is prized for its delicate flavor and subtle hue (white asparagus, a delicacy, is not as common). Crisp, straight, firm stalks with a tight cap are best. Wrap in damp paper towels and refrigerate in a plastic bag for up to 4 days.

BASIL

With its affinity for sauces and tomato-based dishes, it isn't surprising to find basil in many pasta recipes. Intensely aromatic, fresh basil arrives in

ginger root

summer, when tomatoes are at their peak; dried basil may be found on the spice shelf all year. Store freshly cut stems in a little water, cover with plastic, and refrigerate for up to 2 days.

BROCCOLI

Both the rigid green stalks and the tightly packed dark green or purplish-green heads (also called florets) are edible. Choose firm stalks and closed heads with deep color and no yellow areas. Refrigerate in a plastic bag for up to 4 days.

CANNELLINI BEANS

Also known as white kidney beans, these are mild-flavored and meaty when cooked, and available dried or canned. To cook dried cannellini beans, first soak them overnight in cold water, drain and cook in unsalted water for several hours until tender but still keeping their shape.

asparagus

CAPERS

The pickled flower buds of a Mediterranean bush, capers add a piquant note to foods. Most markets stock them in jars with other condiments. Store opened jars in the refrigerator. Before using, drain off their vinegar brine.

CARROTS

Choose firm, bright orange carrots; avoid those that are limp or have cracks or dry spots. Refrigerate in a plastic bag, tops removed, for up to 2 weeks. Peel or scrub before using. Tiny baby carrots are actually a separate variety prized for their delicate flavor and charming appearance. Store them as you would large carrots, but remember their feathery tops will soon wilt.

CHEESES

The following cheeses often appear in pasta dishes. Mascarpone is rich and buttery, a cross between cream cheese and sour cream. Pliable, stringy mozzarella is used in baked dishes and salads. Parmesan is a hard and crumbly grating cheese with a nutty flavor; it is used as the finishing touch on most pasta dishes. Moist ricotta is mild and semisweet, with a soft, creamy texture. Romano is similar to Parmesan, but is sharper in taste. Storage length varies with the type of cheese, but all cheeses must be wrapped well and refrigerated to stay fresh.

artichoke

CHIVES

The long, hollow green leaves of this herb add bright color and a mild onion flavor to many dishes when chopped into pieces. Fresh chives should not be wilted or damaged. Refrigerate, wrapped in damp paper towels and then in a plastic bag, for 3 to 4 days.

FENNEL

With its tubular stalks and feathery leaves, this bulbous, creamy-white to pale-green vegetable resembles celery, but its flavor hints of licorice. Fresh fennel is delicious raw or cooked, while dried fennel seed is used as a seasoning. Select bulbs that are free of cracks or brown spots. Refrigerate in a plastic bag for up to 4 days.

GARLIC

A bulb with a papery outer skin, a head of garlic is composed of numerous small cloves. Garlic may be used as a savory seasoning for almost every course of a meal. It is aromatic and bitter when raw, but becomes delicate and sweet when cooked. Fresh garlic should be plump and firm. Store whole bulbs in a cool, dark, dry place.

GINGER ROOT

The rhizome, or underground stem, of a semitropical plant, fresh ginger root is a pungent seasoning with a lively, hot flavor and peppery aroma. Select stems that are firm and heavy, never shrivelled, with taut, glossy skin. Wrap in a paper towel and refrigerate for up to 2 days. For longer storage, wrap airtight and freeze the unpeeled root.

carrots

KALE

A member of the cabbage family, kale has ruffled dark green leaves and tastes like its cabbage relatives. It is eaten fresh or cooked, or used as a decorative garnish. Wash the leaves in cold water, dry, then refrigerate in a paper towel-lined plastic bag for up to 3 days.

OLIVE OIL

A staple of Mediterranean cooking, olive oil imparts a clean, fruity flavor and golden-to-green color to salad dressings, grilled bread, and pasta sauces. Use extra-virgin oils, from the first pressing, for cold dishes. For sauces, use milder oils that can stand up to heat. Store in a dark spot away from heat for 6 months, or in the refrigerator for a year. (Chilled oil may get thick and cloudy; let it warm to room temperature before using.)

OREGANO

Packed with robust flavor and aroma, oregano is a favorite herb of Italian and Greek cooks. Select bright green fresh oregano with firm stems. Look for dried whole or ground oregano with other spices. Refrigerate fresh oregano in a plastic bag for up to 3 days.

PANCETTA

Unlike regular bacon, mild, spicy-sweet Italian pancetta is rarely smoked, although it is usually seasoned with pepper. It is sold in delicatessens in a roll rather than in a flat slab. Refrigerate it, well wrapped, for several weeks.

PARSLEY

Widely used for cooking and garnish, parsley has such a clean, refreshing flavor that it is sometimes enjoyed as an after-meal digestive. Curly-leaf parsley is mild, while Italian parsley is flat-leafed and more pungent. Select healthy, lively looking bunches.

kale

To store, rinse and shake dry, wrap in paper towels and a
plastic bag, and refrigerate for up to 1 week.

PROSCIUTTO

This spicy, air-dried Italian ham is either eaten raw in paper-
thin slices or heated as part of a recipe. Top-quality prosciutto
di Parma is imported from Italy, but excellent domestic
varieties are also available. Any Italian delicatessen and some
gourmet food shops will stock both types. Wrap and refrigerate
it for several weeks.

olive oils

SQUASH/ZUCCHINI

Soft-skinned, slender green and yellow zucchini (courgettes), straight and crookneck
squashes, and pattypan squashes are classified as "summer" vegetables, although many are sold
year round. They can be used interchangeably. Choose heavy, well-shaped squash without cracks or
bruises. Refrigerate for up to 4 days.

TOMATOES

Botanically a fruit, tomatoes are eaten as a vegetable. Oval-shaped plum tomatoes (also called Italian or
Roma) are thick and meaty, with less juice and smaller seeds than other varieties, which makes them
ideal for sauces. They are sold fresh, or in tins sometimes flavored with basil and other seasonings.
Other tinned or bottled forms include tomatoes cooked with celery, onions, and seasonings; tomato
paste, a highly concentrated purée; and sweet, chewy dried tomatoes, either plain or oil-packed.

Index

Page numbers in *italics* indicate illustrations.

Acknowledgments

Photography Chris Shorten, Kevin Cardland, Rowan Fotheringham
Styling Susan Massey, Vicki Roberts-Russell, Laura Ferguson, Daniel Becker, Jane Hann